ACHIEVING
FINANCIAL STABILITY
in
AMERICA

Misook Yu · CFP®

Achieving Financial Stability in America

Misook Yu, CFP®

Copyright © 2018 by YU & Money Inc.| YUandMoney@Gmail.com

All rights reserved. No part of this book may be reproduced or transmitted in any form or by any means without written permission from the author.

The author has made every effort to ensure the accuracy of the information within this book was correct at time of publication. The author does not assume and hereby disclaims any liability to any party for any loss, damage, or disruption caused by errors or omissions, whether such errors or omissions result from accident, negligence, or any other cause. The author's opinion in this book should not be considered as investment recommendations. Consult qualified professionals for your personal financial matters.

Published in the United States of America
First Edition: [November 2018]
ISBN: [978-1-7320245-1-9] Print
ISBN: [978-1-7320245-1-6] eBook

I dedicate this book to my husband, Terry, without whose full support I wouldn't have been able to go back to school to study finance, quit a job to work for myself, and write this book.

Introduction

Most Americans are in great financial pain. They may appear to be fine because they don't express their suffering, but the overwhelming majority, three out of four, are living paycheck-to-paycheck with less than $1,000 for emergency savings. Many parents are still making payments for their own student loans while scraping every dime to send their children to college at the same time. People with health insurance often hesitate to see a doctor because they fear what they may have to pay under deductible and coinsurance. Seniors are skipping a meal because they can't afford it.

How could that be? Among many reasons, expenses for college education and medical costs have been increasing at a faster rate than inflation, while wages have been stagnating in the past decades. And with decreasing pension plans, people have to prepare for their retirement now, for which they have no training. Financial professionals have been chasing the wealthy for so long, leaving the ordinary people who could've significantly benefited from their service mostly underserved. Many politicians seem to favor policies that are beneficial for their mega-donors, while lip-servicing ordinary people to get their votes. Working hard and being frugal is no longer enough for most people to be financially stable as it had been for the previous generations.

What choice do you, an ordinary person, have to survive in this reality? Save as if your life depends on it and vote for politicians and policies that support *your* financial interests. Learn tax-advantaged features and utilize asset protection rules that have been enjoyed by the wealthy for so long and use them to save, grow, and protect your money. You have more power than you may think to improve your finances, and I hope this book will help awaken that power within you.

For your financial stability,

Misook Yu, CFP®

Table of Contents

CHAPTER 1	**1**
BANKING	**1**
CHECKING ACCOUNT	2
SAVINGS ACCOUNT	5
CD	6
FDIC INSURANCE	7
CHAPTER 2	**10**
CREDIT	**10**
WHY CREDIT MATTERS	11
CREDIT RATING SYSTEM	13
HOW TO BUILD GOOD CREDIT	16
HOW TO FIX ERRORS ON YOUR REPORT	22
CHAPTER 3	**25**
CREDIT CARDS AND LOANS	**25**
CREDIT CARDS	26
LOANS	30
CHAPTER 4	**35**
INSURANCE	**35**
TERM LIFE	36
WHOLE LIFE	39
UNIVERSAL / VARIABLE LIFE	45
ANNUITY	47
HEALTH INSURANCE	51
AUTO INSURANCE	67
HOMEOWNERS INSURANCE	71
OTHER INSURANCE	76
CHAPTER 5	**81**
RETIREMENT PLANNING	**81**
RETIREMENT PROBLEM IN AMERICA	82
WHY RETIREMENT ACCOUNTS?	86
INDIVIDUAL RETIREMENT ACCOUNTS	94
GROUP RETIREMENT PLANS	107

SOCIAL SECURITY	129
RETIREMENT PLANNING	137
OTHER THINGS TO CONSIDER	145

CHAPTER 6 — 154

EDUCATION PLANNING — 154
GRANTS AND SCHOLARSHIPS	155
SAVING FOR COLLEGE	159
STUDENT LOANS	165
EDUCATION PLANNING	172

CHAPTER 7 — 180

INVESTMENT — 180
WHY INVEST?	181
SECURITIES AND INDEX	189
INVESTMENT COSTS	205
HOW TO START SECURITIES INVESTMENT	206

CHAPTER 8 — 211

FINANCIAL ADVISERS — 211
THE REALITY	212
SUITABILITY VS. FIDUCIARY	215
HOW FINANCIAL ADVISERS ARE PAID	217
WHO TO HIRE	219

CHAPTER 9 — 224

PERSONAL BANKRUPTCY — 224
CHAPTER 13 BANKRUPTCY	225
CHAPTER 7 BANKRUPTCY	226
TOP REASONS FOR PERSONAL BANKRUPTCY	228

CHAPTER 10 — 230

PERSONAL TAXES — 230
PAYROLL TAX	231
FEDERAL & STATE INCOME TAX	233
LONG-TERM CAPITAL GAINS TAX	237
AMT (ALTERNATIVE MINIMUM TAX)	238
SALES TAX	240

PROPERTY TAXES	241
ESTATE/GIFT TAX	242
TAX PROBLEMS?	243

CHAPTER 11 — 245

ESTATE PLANNING — 245
IMPORTANCE OF ESTATE PLANNING	246
PROBATE	246
WILL	249
HEALTH CARE DIRECTIVES	251
TRUST	253

CHAPTER 12 — 256

ACHIEVING FINANCIAL STABILITY — 256
FINANCIAL STABILITY	257
SIX STEPS OF FINANCIAL PLANNING	257
FIVE NUMBERS YOU SHOULD KNOW	260
TEN RULES FOR FINANCIAL HEALTH	263
ADVICE BY AGE	268

Chapter 1
BANKING

These days, boundaries between traditional banks and investment companies have largely disappeared, as most banks now offer investment services and investment companies provide banking services. In this chapter, I discuss the basics of banking, regardless of where you open your account.

1. Checking Account
2. Savings Account
3. CD
4. FDIC Insurance

Checking Account

A Checking Account Is Necessary

Checking accounts are used to deposit money and pay bills. Without a checking account, your life can be quite inconvenient, so you should get one when you have income and bills to pay. If you don't have a bank or credit union branch nearby, consider an online bank.

To open a checking account, you typically need a picture ID such as a driver's license or a passport and a proof of address. A bill for your utility, credit card statement, lease agreement, or any similar document can be used. A Social Security number or ITIN is also required. An ITIN (Individual Tax Identification Number) can be obtained by filing IRS Form W-7. See more information on ITIN on IRS.gov (*How Do I Apply for an ITIN?*)

Account Maintenance Fees

Many checking accounts used to be free with no strings attached, but most banks are now charging maintenance fees that can add up to several hundred dollars a year. Check what kinds of fees are charged by the bank you intend to use, and see if you can avoid them. Different banks have different rules and fees, so shop around.

Internet banks tend to offer free or cheaper options for checking accounts because they don't have the expenses that banks with traditional branch offices have. Some people like to go to a local branch office to take care of their business, and some prefer doing everything online. No matter what you prefer, be sure to understand the fine prints to avoid unexpected fees.

If you already have a checking account, see if you are being charged monthly fees. Do not assume that you are not paying any fees just because you've had that account(s) for a long time without being charged. I recently visited a local bank for about five minutes. During that short time, I saw two angry customers who complained about fees that they were not previously paying for holding their account.

Banks may have conditions for free checking accounts, and you need to fully understand them. For example, you may get a free checking account if you have your paycheck automatically deposited into it. But if there is any lapse, say you lose your job and take two months to find another one, then the bank is likely to charge monthly fees during the two months you did not have direct deposits. If this is the case, politely ask your bank's manager to waive the fees.

Other Fees

Two other common fees are ATM fees (charged for using another bank's ATM) and overdraft fees. Overdraft fees are charged when you write a check or make a debit card purchase for more than the cash you have in your account. Most banks provide overdraft protection service - for a fee. And some banks charge for opting out of such service. You also need to pay attention to the order in which your bank clears checks. For example, let's say you have $500 in your checking account. Anticipating a direct paycheck deposit of $1,000 soon, you send out two checks: one for $1,000 and the other for $200. If both checks are deposited before you get paid, the bank may clear the $1,000 first and then the $200, effectively charging two overdraft fees. If it deposits the $200 check first, you'd pay only one overdraft fee, instead of two. It costs you money to miss small details, so protect your money by paying attention. By the way, if you find yourself in a similar situation as the example above, complain to the bank manager and ask for your money back.

Checks

Once you open a checking account, you will be given some temporary checks, and you can order (and pay for) permanent ones with your information such as name and address printed. When writing checks, it is important that you fill out all the areas accurately. If you give a check to an individual for future payment, make sure you write a future date so the recipient won't be able to deposit it earlier. If you forget to sign a check, it won't be accepted at a bank. But if the payment is for recurring payments such as a credit card or utility bills, the company and your bank may accept it.

While many banks offer overdraft protections (meaning even if you don't have money in your account, your bank will clear your check: it is essentially a loan), they may charge a hefty fee for the service. If you aren't using this service and your check has bounced (meaning your bank has refused to transfer money to the depositor), then it *can* become a criminal offense, depending on the amount and the state you live in. Making a habit of documenting and balancing each time you write a check is the best way to avoid the problem.

Debit Card is Not a Credit Card

With your new checking account, you will get a debit card. Most debit cards these days have Visa or MasterCard logo on them, allowing debit cardholders to use them like credit cards. However, there are three significant differences between a debit card and a credit card. First, using a debit card is a modern way of writing a check: purchases you make using a debit card are paid from your checking account, even if you select the "credit" button on the card machine at checkout. Therefore do not use the card if you don't have money in your checking account to cover the purchases. Second, even though you can use your debit card like a credit card, it does not help you build credit. And third, it can be cumbersome to dispute fraudulent activities on debit cards. Debit card transaction disputes can take longer, and there's a risk that you may not fully recover from fraudulent charges, as opposed to credit cards that usually have quicker and better protection on fraudulent activities. It is generally better, in my opinion, to use a credit card for purchases and pay in full each month.

Savings Account

Account for Keeping Emergency Funds

Savings accounts are, as the name implies, for saving. In a savings account, you may keep cash for emergencies or if you expect to use the funds in the near future, say within a few years. Many people who are afraid of losing their hard-earned money in investment tend to prefer saving their money in a savings account. But keeping money that you're planning to use in distant future, say for retirement that is over a decade away, in a "safe" bank account can be a very costly mistake because the money will lose its purchasing power to inflation. Understanding this concept is very important in financial planning, so I'll discuss it throughout the book.

Very Low Interest Earnings

Interest rates are still quite low, historically speaking, so it is not surprising that consumers are earning a historically low interest rate at zero-something percent on their savings accounts (April 2018). Savings and checking accounts are places to safely park your cash for a short amount of time and should not be treated as investment accounts. Therefore, do not expect any "growth" of your money in those accounts. Any interest earnings that you get from these accounts are subject to an ordinary income tax for the year earned. As you should with any other accounts, watch out for *any* fees in your savings account.

CD

Deposit for A Specified Term

A CD (Certificate of Deposit) is often purchased by people who want to secure their principal amount and earn interest income. The way it works is that you lend money to your bank for a specified period and receive a small amount of interest. The term can vary from months to many years, and interest rates are usually higher for CDs with a longer term. Since CD are guaranteed (to a limit) even in the case of a bank failure, the interest rates tend to be lower compared to other financial products such as bonds that do not provide the same protection on the invested principal. Penalties are imposed if you sell CDs earlier than the original term you purchased. So don't buy a five-year CD to get a higher rate when you expect to use the money within one year, for example.

CDs as Long-Term Investment?

Although many individuals with risk aversion favor CDs for "safety," low interest payments that CDs provide hardly make them an efficient vehicle for long-term savings. If you buy a CD that pays an interest rate that is lower than the inflation rate in any given year, for instance, your money actually loses its value. Investment can be "risky" by nature, but most people cannot afford not to invest, in my opinion, because the alternative to not investing, such as keeping money in cash and CDs, is a certain way to lose its value to inflation in the long run. What benefits do you get from keeping your money "safe" if it keeps losing value over time?

FDIC Insurance

Government Guaranteed Insurance

Cash deposits in bank accounts and CDs are insured by the FDIC (Federal Deposit Insurance Corporation) in case of bank failure. The FDIC was created during the Great Depression to restore public trust in the banking system. It is self-funded by the member banks, and no taxpayer money is involved according to FDIC.gov (*When Banks Fail: Facts for Depositors and Borrowers*).

Per Person, Type of Ownership, Institution

If a bank becomes insolvent (fails), the consumers' deposits of up to $250,000 per person per type of ownership and per institution are protected by the FDIC (2018). See the following table to understand how FDIC works.

Person/Ownership/Institution	Sue	John	Bob & Jim
Checking in Bank A	250,000		
CD in Bank B	250,000	500,000	500,000
Saving in Bank A			500,000
Total Deposits	500,000	500,000	1,000,000
FDIC Insured	$500,000	$250,000	$1,000,000

As shown in the table, Sue's total deposits of $500,000 will be protected if both Bank A and Bank B were to fail because she has accounts in two different institutions. All of Bob and Jim's assets of $1,000,000 will be protected as well because they are in a joint account in two different banks. But only 50% of John's $500,000 will be protected because it is in one category (individual ownership) in one institution. John can keep his money FDIC insured either by keeping it in a joint account or depositing $250,000 in two different banks.

Check if Your Bank Is an FDIC Member

Your bank must be a member of the FDIC for your money to be federally protected. Most commercial banks are members, but make sure that you open an account in a member bank. You can ask a bank representative or look for an FDIC sign.

Investment Accounts Are NOT Insured

Be aware that monies that are invested in stocks, mutual funds, bonds, and insurance products are *not* FDIC insured, even if they are in accounts at an FDIC member bank. Items in a safe box in a bank are not insured, either. One thing that can be confusing is money market accounts vs. money market mutual funds in investment accounts: money market accounts are FDIC insured, but money market *mutual funds* are *not*, regardless of where the accounts are held. That is because buying mutual funds is an *investment*, while keeping money in a money market account is considered a *deposit*. Only cash and cash equivalents (checking, savings, CDs, and money market accounts) are FDIC insured. See more information on what is FDIC insured and what is not on FDIC.gov. (*Insured or Not Insured?*).

Chapter 2
CREDIT

Bad credit can cost a lot of money throughout one's life. You can pay higher interest rates on loans, and insurance can be more expensive. It can also affect your job prospects because most employers pull the applicants' credit. Understand how credit can affect your overall life and take good care of it.

1. Why Credit Matters
2. Credit Rating System
3. How to Build Good Credit
4. How to Fix Errors on Your Report

Why Credit Matters

Bad Credit Can Cost You a Lot of Money

I cannot stress enough how much credit can affect your life because it can save or cost you a lot of money for the same purchase or service. If you have lower credit scores than what credit card companies or banks like, then they will charge you higher interest rates on your credit card or a loan.

MarketWatch.com reports that the average rate on used car loans is 8.56%, compared to 4.46% for new cars (*Why Used-Car Loans are Clunkers*). The average rate for the people with the poorest credit scores was a whopping 17.72%, which means that those people who get used car loans pay too much for inferior cars. This article was written in 2013, so you can expect the rates should be higher now in 2018 because interest rates have risen since then. This shows how people with bad credit have to pay dearly for the same or similar purchase.

 The bigger problem that can be the beginning of one's financial ruin occurs when his or her car breaks down before the loan is paid off. Let's assume that you got a used car two years ago with a five-year loan, and the engine failed today. You don't have money to get a new engine or cannot borrow from anyone. Even if you can borrow the money today, you know you won't be able to pay it back anytime soon. If you don't go to work tomorrow, you're jeopardizing your employment. What choice do you have here? In desperation, many people go back to a used car dealership where they know they can get another car immediately. Since you still owe thousands of dollars on your worthless old vehicle, you have no choice but to consolidate the old loan with the new one for *another* used car. I have seen people paying over $1,000 a month, which is almost half of their paycheck, on a used car that is worth maybe a few thousand dollars in resale value. You can quickly fall into this trap if you go through a few used cars that give you trouble before the loan is paid off. At this point, you are in a financial black hole that you may not be able to get out of, even if you keep working full-time until retirement. The sad reality is that more and more Americans are falling into this trap because their income hasn't increased as much as living costs have over decades.

Good Credit = Savings and More

People with good credit can save money in various ways. Let's say you and your friend with similar income each buy a house with a 30-year, $300,000 mortgage, for example. If your interest rate is fixed at 4% and payments are made as originally scheduled, you'd pay about $516,000 for principal and interest. But if your friend with less-than-optimal credit has a rate fixed at 5%, he'd pay a total of about $579,000. That is more than a $60,000 difference! Your friend is likely to pay higher interest payments on other loans and insurance premiums. Even his job prospects can be negatively affected because employers typically consider applicants' credit when they hire new people. The bottom line is that people with good credit can save money in many ways, allowing them to save more. That would help them financially advance much farther than those with bad credit.

Let me be blunt: having bad credit sucks in many ways. Bad credit makes your loans more expensive, which makes it harder for you to save.

It is also humiliating to deal with loan officers acting as if they are doing you a favor by "giving" you a loan with a high interest rate that they'd get a fat commission from. But if you have excellent credit, on the other hand, it is a different world because life gets much easier and nicer. You can choose which lender to use for your loans, and salespeople will do their best to get your business, assuming no issues on your ability to repay. Even if someone is not kind to you for whatever reason, you have options to go to other places that will welcome you. Having such options gives you powers to get better deals throughout your life, which further enables you to accumulate more wealth. Good credit is a vital building block for financial stability.

Credit Rating System

3 Credit Bureaus

There are three credit bureaus that collect consumers' credit data: Equifax, Experian, and Trans Union. Despite the names (credit "bureaus" or credit "agencies"), they are not government agencies or nonprofit organizations. They are for-profit companies whose practices are subject to some government regulations. The companies gather consumers' payment histories and use them to calculate their credit scores. Companies are not obligated to report their customers' payment history to credit bureaus, and the credit bureaus don't share information with one another as a general business practice. Since it costs money for companies to report to credit bureaus, small companies may choose to report to only one, while some may not report to any. That is why FICO scores are often different between companies.

Chapter 2 | CREDIT

3-Digit FICO Scores

Most commonly used credit scores called FICO (Fair Isaac and Company) ranges between 300-850, and they are categorized as followed: Poor (under 580), Fair (580-669), Good (670-739), Very Good (740-799), and Excellent (800+). Less frequently used credit score is VantageScore ranging from 501-990, but I focus on FICO in this book.

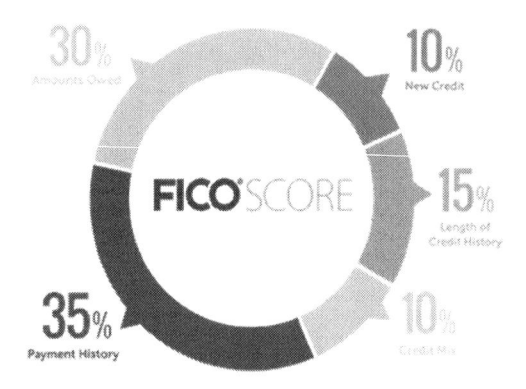

(Source: MyFICO.com)

The graph above was pulled early 2018, and FICO score calculations are to change starting 2019 to incorporate banking information, which is expected to include banking information. I'll update it in the next edition, so use this information to understand basics of the scoring system. As shown on the graph, payment history (35%) is the most crucial area, followed by amounts owed (30%) and length of credit history (15%). These three make up 80% of one's FICO score. When you think about it, building good credit requires common sense: minimize borrowing and make payments on time. Many people are eager to chase after "good deals" and frequently open/close credit accounts. They may be able to save some money by doing it, but that does not help build good credit, as 15% of one's FICO score is determined by the length of credit history.

25% Errors in Credit Report

According to a study conducted by the Federal Trade Commission (ftc.gov) in 2013, one in four (25%) consumers found at least one error in their credit reports, and 5% found an error that could cause them to pay a higher interest rate in a loan (*In FTC Study, Five Percent of Consumers Had Errors on Their Credit Reports That Could Result in Less Favorable Terms for Loans*). The error rate is shockingly high, which is why it is critical to check your credit reports for accuracy.

Seven Years of Records

Most credit information including late payments and Chapter 13 bankruptcies stay for seven years. Chapter 7 bankruptcies and most judgments such as liens and settlements may stay up to 10 years, although it may differ by states. Simple mistakes or errors on your credit report can ruin your credit scores in a short time, but recovering can take many years. Thus always pay attention to what's on your credit, especially before you apply for a loan.

Free Credit Report Every Year

You can check your credit report from all three credit bureaus for *free* every 12 months on AnnualCreditReport.com or by calling 1-877-322-8228. You can also print out the Annual Credit Report Request Form from the website and mail it.

The FTC (Federal Trade Commission) advises not to contact the three nationwide credit-reporting companies individually, as they are providing free annual credit reports only through the ways explained above. When getting your free report online, watch out for imposters that sound similar to the name of the website. For security and identification purposes, you'll be asked to answer questions that only you would know, such as your Social Security number and the amount of your monthly loan payment. For more information regarding free credit reports, visit AnnualCreditReport.com or the Federal Trade Commission's website (Consumer.FTC.gov).

How to Build Good Credit

What Shows on Credit Reports

Reporting to credit bureaus is not mandatory for companies, as stated previously, but you should expect that anything you have related to loans and payments is on your report. It shows amounts of debts on loans, whether there have been any late payments or delinquencies, and if there are any civil judgments including tax liens or unpaid child support payments. Credit cards, TV subscriptions, phone bills, and mortgage or lease payments are some examples that many people who live independently have. Utility bills that are paid on time are not typically reported, but delinquent utility bills are likely to be shown on your report.

Pay Bills on Time (Automate It)

First and foremost, pay bills on time in *full*. Your payment history makes up 35% of your FICO score. Setting up automatic payments is the best way to be on time, in my opinion. Most banks allow customers to set up free automatic payments, so use them. If you are not comfortable with technology, this is one thing that I strongly suggest you learn, even if you have to pay someone. Set up auto payment using your credit card for billers such as phone and cable TV companies who don't charge extra fees. Most utility companies charge a fee for credit card processing, so avoid it by making payments from your checking account. I set up my regular payments via online banking, including utility bills and mortgage payments. All my other bills such as phone and the Internet service that accept credit card payments without any fee are set up to be charged to my credit card. My credit card payments are, of course, automatically paid from my checking account as well. This simple automatic payment setup via online banking and a credit card eliminates possibilities of being late. I also set up automatic alerts so I can receive a text message every time there's any activity on my credit card and bank accounts. I hope you'll use this technology to your advantage and watch your account activities closely.

Not Too Many, Not Too Few Accounts

Credit accounts you own make up 30% of your FICO score. Having too many credit accounts is not a good idea for many reasons. But having too few credit accounts is not helpful in building good credit, either. Some people don't like borrowing, so they save up money and buy things with cash, including cars and even houses. While it may be a financially responsible behavior, it is hard for the credit bureaus to analyze and compute your "trustworthiness," if you don't have credit accounts. That can hurt you because your credit affects you in other ways such as determining insurance premiums or getting a job.

I encourage people to use the system to their advantage by buying things using a credit card(s) and paying it off each month. Alternatively, you could take out a loan for a car instead of paying cash, even if you had that much cash saved. There's no specific number of credit accounts that are supposed to be the "best," but having mixed accounts such as a combination of one credit card, a car loan, and a mortgage, for example, is desirable, compared to three credit cards or two car loans only. 10% of your FICO score is calculated based on the types of accounts you have established.

Keep Low Credit Utilization Rate

One of the ways to measure how you can "control" yourself, therefore exhibiting your financial responsibility is to see your credit utilization rate, which is calculated as followed:

Credit utilization rate = Credit card balance ÷ Credit limit

For example, if your credit card limit is $3,000 and your average balance is $2,000, then your credit utilization rate is 67% ($2,000/$3,000 = 0.67 or 67%) If you have more than one credit card, then they are combined for the calculation. Let's say you have another credit card with a $2,000 limit and average balance of $500; then, your credit utilization rate is 50% [($2,000+$500) /($3,000+$2,000) = 0.5 or 50%]

There is no one "the best" utilization rate for excellent credit scores. Less than 33% is desirable in general, while some argue for only one digit rate. I try to keep mine around 20-30%. The credit utilization rate is calculated based on the date that your credit card company reports to the credit card bureaus. I don't know or care when my card companies report to credit bureaus. That is because when I purchase a large item that would raise my credit utilization rate considerably higher, I make an immediate payment without waiting for the statement. Unlike other parts of the

FICO system, this is a quick and easy way to boost your credit score, and you are in total control. Keep your credit utilization rate low at all times.

Age of Credit Accounts Matters

Typically, most credit information stays on your credit report for seven years, and the longer positive history you have, the better. Each time you acquire credit (apply for a credit card or a loan), it negatively affects your credit and stays on your record for two years; therefore, do not take "special offers" every time you're offered a discount at checkout. Having two accounts current (meaning no late payments) for five years is better than opening/closing two accounts each year, for example. The length of credit history contributes 15% of your FICO score.

Secured Personal Loan

If you want to build credit beyond a few credit cards, you can consider getting a personal loan from a bank. Tell the banker that you intend to build credit and ask what it takes to get a small loan. Most banks are likely to loan you a 12-month loan against a CD. How does this work? You can buy a $2,000 CD, borrow the same or a smaller amount against the CD, and pay the loan over a year or so with interest. Yes, it costs you money for interest payments, but it may be worth paying to build credit relatively fast if a lack of credit accounts is an issue for you.

Do Not Co-sign

You may be asked to co-sign for a car loan or an apartment lease by your family member or friend. Do not co-sign unless you are willing and able to assume the financial responsibility. Of course, we want to help our loved ones when we can, but co-signing comes with legal and financial liability. Once you co-sign for a loan, it is on your credit, meaning if the original borrower/renter is late making payments, your credit is damaged as well, and you can be responsible for the loan at the end. If you are not willing to assume the loan or cannot afford the payments, do not co-sign for *anyone*. Likewise, do not ask people to co-sign for you, either. If you do co-sign for any reason, however, I suggest you receive money from the original borrower and make payments to the lender directly. It is the only way to protect your credit and help the person build credit at the same time, in my opinion.

Know What Affects Credit More

Larger payments such as mortgage loans and car payments tend to affect credit more than smaller ones. Recent payments count for more than older ones. Payments you make because you owe such as loans affect your credit, but those you pay for service in advance such as insurance premiums don't. Understand that the consequence of not paying insurance premiums is that you lose your coverage, which is bad because driving without it is illegal. I'm just explaining how things can affect your credit.

When money is tight, negotiate so you can minimize the negative impact on your credit. Proactively contact creditors as soon as you realize there may be a problem. Ask if they will temporarily accept partial payments. Be honest and polite no matter the results. The better your credit history with certain creditors, the better the chance they will work with you.

If things don't work out in your favor, you need to prioritize payments. Making partial payments (even without permission from the creditors) may delay the creditors from reporting to credit bureaus. There's no one correct answer in prioritizing payments because people's needs and risks differ. Whatever decision you make, do it with a goal to protect your credit.

Protect Your Credit

You've probably heard of hacking at Target (a large retail store) and Equifax (one of the credit bureaus). In this digital age we live in, all personal information and digital transactions are saved in companies and organizations that we use. Hacking at one place, especially a credit bureau whose business is to collect personal financial data, can expose all of our sensitive personal information such as Social Security number, date of birth, and address. With that information, fraudulent accounts in your name can be opened without your knowledge. When it comes to credit card fraud in which someone steals your credit card number and makes purchases, it is relatively easy to fix the problem. However, if someone obtains a loan in your name, it can give you a nightmare before you can have it dissolved. One proactive way to stop that from happening is to freeze your credit. Once you freeze your credit, no one, including yourself, can apply for a credit account until you lift the freeze. Credit bureaus used to charge $5-$10 each time you freeze or unfreeze your credit until recently but they do not anymore. This proactive and free step is more effective than any credit monitoring service, which is reactive and not free.

How to Fix Errors on Your Report

No Magic Wand

There is no magic wand that can fix one's bad credit or erroneous credit report quickly. There are many "professionals" who promise to fix your bad credit fast, but you can do everything they do for free. The truth is that you have to know what's in your credit and provide all the supporting documents to help them understand your situation so they can work for you, anyway., so you might as well do it yourself and save money. Besides saving money, I firmly believe that people should take charge of such an important matter that affects their life significantly.

Disputing

Fixing an error is not difficult, though it may take some time for it to be removed from your credit report. The first step is to identify any error(s) on your credit report from all three credit bureaus. Once identified, gather supporting documents. If a debt amount is overstated, for example, you can send a copy of a correct statement from the creditor. The following letter is a sample from Federal Trade Commission website (*Sample Letter for Disputing Errors on Your Credit Report*):

[Your Name]
[Your Address]
[Your City, State, Zip Code]
[Date]
Complaint Department
[Company Name] [Street Address] [City, State, Zip Code]
Dear Sir or Madam:

I am writing to dispute the following information in my file. I have marked the items I dispute on the attached copy of the report I received.

This item [identify item(s) disputed by name of source, such as creditors or tax court, and identify type of item, such as credit account, judgment, etc.] is [inaccurate or incomplete] because [describe what is inaccurate or incomplete and why]. I am requesting that the item be removed [or request another specific change] to correct the information.

Enclosed are copies of [use this sentence if applicable and describe any enclosed documentation, such as payment records and court documents] supporting my position. Please reinvestigate this [these] matter[s] and [delete or correct] the disputed item[s] as soon as possible.

Sincerely,
Your name
Enclosures: [List what you are enclosing.]

Record Keeping

Keep copies of all the documents you send and use certified mail with the required signature when sending documents so you can later verify the delivery. Keep all communication in writing, whether it is US mail or email. If you have a phone conversation, keep a good record of it including time and names. Make a master file so you can easily keep track of the process.

What Happens Next

Once your dispute is received, the credit bureau(s) must open an investigation, usually within 30 days. They must contact the parties involved and forward the information. Once the investigation is complete, they must notify you of the result in writing, along with a free credit report. If your dispute is successfully resolved, it must be shared with all other credit bureaus for necessary correction(s). You can ask the credit bureau(s) to send a notice of correction to anyone who obtained your credit in the past six months. For employment related parties, it is past two years. See more information on this topic on FTC.gov (*Disputing Errors on Credit Reports*)

Be Patient and Professional

Correcting errors on your credit can take a long time, often months. It can be frustrating, but always be patient and professional. If you feel that the person on the other side is not competent, politely ask to speak to his or her supervisor. Keep a record of any related activity in detail.

Chapter 3
CREDIT CARDS AND LOANS

Credit cards are essential for building good credit and make your life convenient in general. Loans are necessary for people to make big purchases such as a car and a house. Most Americans cannot afford the college education without taking students loans. But as essential as credit cards and loans are in American life, they can ruin one's finance if not carefully managed.

1. Credit Cards
2. Loans

Credit Cards

Types of Credit Cards

Credit cards can be categorized in several ways such as who issues them, whether they have rewards or not, whether they are secured or not, and so on. Regardless of who issues, the majority of credit cards go through one of the four networks in the US: VISA, MasterCard, American Express, and Discover, in the order of total processed volume from high to low.

As for secured credit cards, they are typically used by people with lower credit scores. They are like debit cards in a way that you have to have cash in your account to be able to use it. The difference is that using debit cards doesn't help credit history while using secured credit cards does.

Be Aware of Fees and Avoid Them

As with any financial product, you need to be aware of fees. There are credit cards that have an annual membership fee, although some may waive it for the first year, but there are many without a membership fee. No fancy benefits are worth paying for if you don't use them. Evaluate how useful member benefits are for you before getting a card with an annual fee.

Interest rates are an important factor that requires close attention when you choose a credit card. Typical interest rates on most cards vary from about 10% to over 25% per year. I hope you pay off the balance each month without having to pay an interest payment, but even with the best intentions, you may fall behind occasionally. The interest rate matters a lot in that case, so always try to get a card with the lowest rate possible. You can ask the card company to lower it, though you may or may not get it. Also, pay attention to other fees such as late payment fees, foreign transaction fees, cash advance fees, returned payment fee, etc. Fees here and there can quickly add up, so avoid them if you can. Ask the company to waive whatever charge or penalty you may occasionally accrue. You may be surprised by what you can get by merely asking.

Take Advantage of Rewards

Card rewards such as cash back and airline mileage are popular among cardholders. Cash back rewards are as straightforward as they sound: you get a certain percentage (typically 1%) of your spending back in cash. You can then use it to pay down your balance, donate it, or get gift cards at partnering businesses.

Airline mileages can be used to book a flight or for other travel bookings such as hotels and car rentals. Make sure that you understand how it works and what you can use the miles for. I once had a mileage card but canceled it after realizing there were many limitations on when I could use them. For example, some days required more miles than others or were not available for mileage booking at all. I now mainly use two credit cards that give me 1% cash back on every purchase plus 5% on specific purchases (different each month). With the accumulated bonus points, I get gift cards at a 10-20% discount from my credit card company's network partners. I go to movies, eat out, and shop with those gift cards. I seldom pay for my clothes out of pocket, granted that I don't shop much.

Shopping with gift cards that I didn't pay for is exciting, but those bonus points could be accumulated only when I use my credit cards (spend money). You'd be surprised by how many people pay more attention to rewards than spending itself; therefore, earn your rewards and enjoy them however you want, but don't be blindsided by "rewards." You wouldn't spend $100 cash to get a $1 reward, would you?

There are many other card member benefits such as roadside assistance, travel insurance, and amusement park discounts, to name a few. Carefully view them and choose the cards that can be most useful for you.

Be Aware of "Special Deals"

Many retail stores offer "special discounts" such as 20% off if you apply for their credit card at the checkout. "No Payment & No Interest Until 20xx" is another tempting advertisement for furniture. Remember that every time you apply to get any credit card or a loan, it negatively impacts your credit score, so make your decision after careful consideration of the pros and cons before biting at any deal. I usually recommend rejecting those "deals," unless you need more credit accounts to build the credit history. Even when it makes sense to ding a little bit of your credit score to get an irresistible deal, try to time it so you won't do it right before you get a larger purchase such as a home.

Rolling Over Debts

Credit card statements show a small amount of "minimum payment" as if that is all you need to pay. If you don't pay the whole amount in full each month, the unpaid balance essentially becomes a loan with a high interest rate, depending on your card. If you make only minimum payments, which are about 1-2% of the total balance, it can take decades for you to pay that off. Overdue interest payments, fees, and penalties can quickly compound and double the original debt in a matter of a few years.

If you already have credit card debt you struggle to pay, offers for a balance transfer with "special rate" may look like a savior. Transferring balance could be a good strategy to lower your credit card interest, but pay close attention to fees and the interest rate that you'll have to pay *after* the attractive introductory rate ends. Card companies offer eye-popping 0% or an extremely low interest rate because they are betting that people would not be able to pay the balance in full during that introductory rate and end up paying high rates. If you are not sure if transferring the balance to another credit card makes financial sense, consulting a financial adviser may be worth the money, especially if you have a large debt.

Of course, not carrying any credit card balance is the best practice because if you do, that means you are paying at least 10%, but closer to 20% or more of the total amount each year. So don't be fooled by the minimum payment amount, and always pay the entire balance in full.

Supporting Local Businesses

I don't like using cash in general because it is much more convenient to use a card. Plus, I enjoy getting bonus rewards that come from my credit cards. Have you wondered, by the way, how credit card companies offer such sweet rewards? They get their money from the stores where you shop. Whenever you pay with a credit card, your credit card company charges a percentage of the total sales from the merchant for the transaction. The card companies that offer higher rewards to their customers tend to charge higher transaction fees. Small business owners don't have the same bargaining power as national retail chains do regarding credit card processing fees. They pay higher average merchant fees than large companies do, which is why some small merchants set a minimum amount to pay with a card or accept cash only. For penny-squeezing small businesses, such fees can threaten their existence, which is why I try to use cash when shopping at local businesses or any store that I like. I'm willing to forgo my 1% reward point by paying cash, so my favorite local stores can save 3-4% (or more) in card processing fees and stay in business longer for me and my community. I thought it'd be worth mentioning, in case you also want to support your favorite businesses.

Loans

Student Loan

Student loans are a big part of going to college in America because colleges and universities are very expensive. It is not uncommon that parents continue to make their own student loan payments even until their children go to college. Unlike consumer loans such as credit card debts or car loans, student loans are difficult to be forgiven even through personal bankruptcy. That is one of the reasons that it is relatively easier to get student loans compared to other consumer loans. You should take student loans with extreme caution. I wrote a separate section dedicated to student loans, as I believe they require more explanation. See Chapter 6 "Education Planning" for more information on student loans.

Home Loan

A typical mortgage is 15 or 30-year fixed, but other terms and adjustable rates are available. I generally prefer a fixed-rate mortgage for simplicity. Do not fall for any "creative" lending practices and be sure to read the fine print. Low or no down payment for a mortgage may sound attractive, though it is not as commonly offered as it was before the recent financial crisis.

If you put less than 20% down for your home purchase, you may be required to buy private mortgage insurance (PMI), though there are some exceptions with government-sponsored mortgages. PMI is insurance that protects the lender, not the borrower who pays the premium, in case of the borrower's default. It is separate from homeowners insurance and ranges around 0.5-1.0% of a loan amount. For example, if you buy a house with 5% down and borrow $300,000, then you can expect to pay extra $1,500-$3,000 per year for PMI on top of the mortgage interest and principal payments, homeowners insurance, and property taxes. Once your loan-to-value ratio drops to lower than 80%, ask the lender to drop the PMI, as they may not be motivated to cancel it proactively.

Try to avoid interest-only payment loans, too. You never build equity on your home through these loans, and you can be hit very hard when the housing market goes down or the rate increases. Anything that allows you to buy a house without a 20% down payment can often be a potential recipe for financial trouble down the road.

During the Great Recession about a decade ago, some 10 million Americans lost their homes. Many things are to blame for it: the bad economy that depressed home prices and caused people to lose their jobs, unethical lending practices by lenders who gave loans without income verification, and borrowers who took loans that they could not afford in the first place. The economy is now said to have recovered and continues to grow with historically low unemployment rates, but many individuals are still paying dearly for their losses. Strong growth of stock markets didn't help them increase assets because they didn't have money to invest in the market, and the low unemployment rate hasn't provided them with higher income.

Since preventing such a crisis from repeating requires much political, ethical, and economic efforts, we should defend our finances all we can first. That means taking care of credit, having at least a 20% down payment when buying a home, and living below means and saving more. Have homeowners insurance and property taxes included in the mortgage payments, so your monthly budgets are consistent. Get a fixed mortgage instead of one with an adjustable interest rate, especially these days when interest rates are relatively low.

Don't buy as big of a house as a lender is willing to lend you. A 15-year fixed mortgage will have higher monthly payments, but the interest rate will be lower than a 30-year mortgage and you can pay off the loan faster. I don't have a problem with a 30-year mortgage, but I want you to use a 15-year mortgage as a test of your financial ability to buy a house: If you are qualified only for a 30-year mortgage, but not a 15-year one, for the home you want, that is a good indication that you may be stretching your money more than you should. When you stretch your finances too much to buy a home without a realistic prospect for higher income in the near future, you put yourself in danger of missing payments even with little financial stress. It is highly likely that property taxes and homeowners insurance premiums will continue to go up in the future, and your house will naturally need repairs as it ages. Therefore, expect that your overall cost of home ownership will increase, and please give yourself a financial cushion by getting a smaller mortgage than the maximum loan that lenders are willing to offer you.

Shop around. Be sure to check with at least three lenders when you buy your home, even if you know your credit is not great. I find searching and comparing quotes on the Internet easier because all the communication is documented, and it is less time-consuming (I can get several quotes in one inquiry, for example).

Auto Loan

Auto loans usually have lower rates when obtained through the financial branch of an auto manufacturer, but you should, of course, shop around. I've seen too many people with a steady job but with less-than-perfect credit getting into a financial black hole because they assume that they cannot get a loan from a reputable lender and not shop around. Many don't even visit banks. Instead, they go with whoever first offers a loan. Please do not assume anything until you check with at least three banks. Credit unions and local banks may be more lenient in loan availabilities for people with lower credit ratings. Be patient and shop around. If you already have an auto loan with a high interest rate, see if you can refinance it with someone else, but watch out for fees.

Predatory Lending

In the era where the overwhelming majority of Americans live paycheck-to-paycheck, it is not surprising that so many people are falling prey to predatory lending. In many cases, people who go to a predatory lender have bad credit and won't be able to borrow from a bank. Even for people with decent credit and the ability to repay, banks are often hard to find in their low-income area, leaving them no choice but to use predatory lenders occasionally.

Payday loans are one of the most common short-term loans. Rates on these loans are astronomical at 390% to 780% APR, according to PaydayLoanInfo.org (*How Payday Loans Work*). Another commonly used short-term loan is a title loan. People who need urgent cash can go to a lender with the title of their property, whether it is a car or home, and put it up as collateral. Although it is technically a secured loan, the interest rate is extremely high. NBCNews.com reports that an average title loan borrower borrows $950 and ends up paying $2,140 over a ten-month period (*Pay $2,140 to borrow $950? That is how car title loans work*). I don't feel it is even necessary for me to explain why you should avoid predatory lenders at all cost.

Chapter 4
INSURANCE

Insurance plays an integral role in protecting finances in cases of unexpected events such as sickness, accidents and premature death. Understanding the benefits and reducing costs is the key to protection and saving. Pay particular attention to details on complex insurance products.

1. Term Life
2. Whole Life
3. Universal/Variable Life
4. Annuity
5. Health Insurance
6. Auto Insurance
7. Homeowners Insurance
8. Other Insurance

Term Life

Coverage for Limited Time and No Cash Value

Term life insurance is simple. It pays death benefits (face value) upon the death of an insured for a specified period and has no cash value. For example, if I purchase a 20-year term life policy with $200,000 face value today, my beneficiary will receive that amount if I were to die within 20 years. If I don't, the policy expires, and the insurance company gets to keep all the premium that I have paid. If I cancel it before the 20-year contract is up, I don't get any money back.

Low Premiums

Premiums on term life insurance policies are significantly lower than other life insurance products that are more complex and have cash value. For example, a healthy nonsmoking male age 40 can get a 20-year term insurance policy with $500,000 of coverage for only $30-$40 per month, according to InstantQuoteLifeInsurance.com. Premiums for younger and healthy people are cheaper. Women are also cheaper to insure than men of the same age, but older people and those with less-than-optimal health conditions will pay higher premiums. Most insurance companies will check your health and medical records before issuing you a life insurance policy. They can increase a proposed premium or even deny any coverage based on their findings.

Level premiums are the most popular payment method because the amount is the same each month or year during the contract term. If a policy has increasing premium, the owner makes small payments in the beginning and the premiums increase over time, and vice versa. I generally recommend level premium policies because it makes budgeting easy.

How Much Insurance to Purchase

How much life insurance you need depends on your circumstances and goals. If you don't have any loved ones who would financially suffer in case of your premature death, you may not need life insurance, but if you have anyone who financially depends on you, then you do need one. For the insurance amount you require, multiply what you need by time. For instance, if you want to protect your surviving family that requires $50,000 per year for 10 years, you can buy a 10-year $500,000 policy. For a more comprehensive calculation based on your specific needs and circumstances, you can use an online calculator such as Bankrate.com (*Life Insurance Calculator*). You can always buy more insurance than you need, but keep in mind that term policies don't have cash values. I recommend buying enough insurance to cover what you need and concentrate on saving. Your insurance policies should be reviewed and updated as your situations change over time.

How to Buy

Thanks to the simplicity of term life insurance, it is easy to compare premiums online. If you prefer to sit down with an agent, understand that you may need to pay for that convenience, meaning likely higher premiums than online quotes. Regardless of your preference, be sure to get several quotes from different companies and compare them before purchasing one.

The financial health of insurance companies is something that you also should pay attention to. A.M. Best is an agency (privately held company) that specializes in rating insurance companies' overall financial health and ability to pay claims. Their ratings are A++, A+, A, A-, B++, B+, B, B-... and so on. I prefer insurance companies with A or higher rating by A.M. Best.

Do Not Lie

Do not lie on the application, as insurance companies can deny payments based on that. If you didn't state your risky hobby of skydiving on the application and died from it, for example, the insurance company is likely to deny paying your beneficiaries. If you neglect to state a health problem on your application and died from a car accident, the company can still deny the claim, even though the material misstatement on the application didn't have anything to do with the actual cause of death. Insurance companies can also adjust (reduce) benefit payouts based on their final discoveries. They exist to make money, and they will do their best to maximize their profits, minimizing payouts if at all possible. Honesty is the best policy to avoid potential problems, so do not misstate or lie on the application.

Read the Fine Print

Like anything else, it is important you understand what you buy. Carefully read the fine print before signing any document and understand exclusions in your policy. Do not let any agent rush you into signing anything before you fully understand the policy. Suicides within a few years of obtaining the policy, epidemics, and death in war are usually excluded in life insurance.

How to Use Term Life Insurance

As you know, term policies allow you to buy a death benefit at a low price for a limited time, and they don't have cash values. So I believe that an effective way to use term life is to buy what you need and save the money you otherwise would've paid for whole life insurance. For example, say you have two options: a 20-year $500,000 term insurance for $35 a month and a whole life policy with the same death benefit for $500 a month. Then you can buy a term policy and invest $465 per month. Along with other retirement savings, you should have approximately $500,000 by the time your term life policy expires in 20 years, so you won't "need" life insurance anymore.

Whole Life

Lifetime Coverage + Cash Value

Whole life insurance is permanent, as opposed to term life insurance that lasts a limited time such as 10 or 20 years. As the name indicates, a whole life insurance policy covers the lifetime of the insured until death or the policy's maturity, which used to be about 100 years of age but now is about 120. The maturity of a policy at age 120 means that if an insured survives until age 120, the owner, not the beneficiary, of the policy gets the insurance face value. At this point, the payment becomes a taxable disbursement in which any profits beyond the premiums paid are subject to taxes.

Whole life insurance consists of two components: life insurance and savings. Premiums on whole life insurance are expensive because it covers the entire life of the insured, as opposed to term life insurance that covers a limited period. Premiums can be made as a single premium or fixed payments over time. The savings portion has a guaranteed growth rate that is lower than the average securities market growth. Death benefits (face values) are fixed.

Complex and Expensive

Unlike term life insurance, which is straightforward, whole life insurance is complex with many features that are available at additional costs. Disability income, premium waiver for disability, term conversion, accelerated death benefits, and guaranteed insurability are some examples of riders that policyholders can get on their whole life insurance. If some features that sound good come as standard, then the costs are already built into the premium.

Death Benefit Is Fixed

Like term life, a death benefit in whole life insurance is fixed. It is essential that you fully understand what a fixed death benefit means. Assume that you, at age 45, are thinking of buying a whole life policy with a $500,000 death benefit, for example. This amount may sound like a lot of money to you now, but if you live a full life, say until 85, then how much would it be worth in 40 years? With a modest 2% inflation rate estimation, today's $500,000 insurance would be worth only about $223,000 in 40 years. If the future inflation rate is to be over 3% like the historical average rate for the past many decades had been, today's

$500,000 would be worth a little over $100,000 in 40 years. We don't know what future inflation rates will be, but it is safe to say that the longer you live, the less a fixed death benefit (or any fixed amount, for that matter) would be worth in the future.

Commission and Surrender Charges

Commission to agents is a big part of costs in whole life insurance products, running 30-90% of the first year's premiums. (Investopedia.com: *Becoming an Insurance Agent*) It can be as high as 130-150%, according to ConsumerReports.org (*Is Whole Life Insurance Right For You?*). Moreover, agents often receive a percentage of residual commission every year, as long as the premiums are paid. Commission structure varies by type of agents, products, and different companies. The more commission and other fees are paid, the longer it takes for the policy owner to accumulate cash value in whole life insurance.

Insurance companies don't usually profit in the beginning years mainly due to commission payouts. That is why they impose surrender charges, which are penalties that policyholders must pay if they terminate a policy within a specified period. Depending on the policy, this period can be more than 10 years, and I've recently seen one with a 20-year surrender charge.

Loan

When you accumulate enough cash value in your policy, usually after your policy is no longer subject to a surrender charge, you can borrow against it. Since it is a loan, you don't pay tax on the amount, *and* you don't have to pay it back, unlike any other loans. Sounds good, right?

But understand that you're not withdrawing some portion of *your* cash value; instead, you are borrowing from the insurance company with your cash value as collateral. The interest rate on a loan is often higher than the rate your cash value earns. Sure, you don't have to pay it back in theory, but the reality is that the interest portion keeps accumulating, and the unpaid principal and accrued interest amount is deducted from the cash value or death benefit. Depending on the loan amount and how long you don't make loan payments, your beneficiary may get a minimal amount at the end.

Life Insurance on Children?

You can buy a rider for a little extra amount that covers your children's life on your policy. Insurance companies market this rider for 'savings' that your child can tap later and they also guarantee insurability in case your children get sick. No matter how good they sound, I generally oppose life insurance on children. Life insurance is designed to save surviving family members from financial catastrophe in case of an insured's premature death. You are not going to be hurt financially if your young child were to die before you. I understand tragedies happen and funerals are expensive. That is why you must have emergency funds saved that is enough to cover at least three to six months' worth of your essential expenses. If you still think a child life rider is a good idea for "savings" that he or she can later tap, how about investing the money into a tax-advantaged education account, instead?

Shop Around

Premiums on whole life insurance can vary widely depending on products and companies. Shop around and compare many quotes before purchasing one. Insurance products that you buy from local agents are typically more expensive than what you can get online, although many brokers/agents seem to offer comparable quotes these days. If you have a friend or family who you want to buy a policy from, shop around first and ask him or her to match the price. Ask what amount of your premium goes toward your investment and cash value, as opposed to other costs. It is not necessarily to find out how much they make (although you should know how much commission you're paying the agent) but rather to understand how much it will cost you to buy a product. It is your money and your right. Insurance products are often too complicated for most people to understand fully. You should at least know how much of what you're paying is being saved or invested for you.

You may wonder why I emphasize fees so much. That is because, unlike other consumer products, financial products can affect your finance throughout your lifetime. If you pay more than average on a washer, for example, it doesn't change your finance much in the long run. But small differences in fees on financial products like whole life insurance, mortgage, and investment can reduce your wealth significantly because they are paid over decades. That is why you should pay attention to fees when you buy financial products or hire a financial adviser.

Insurance as Investment?

In case you haven't noticed, I'm not a big fan of whole life insurance in general. I don't think those fancy features are worth the costs for most people, especially for those who don't (can't) save to the maximum limits on their qualified retirement accounts. You may argue that investment is too risky, and the guaranteed principal protection in whole life insurance is desirable. I understand, but at what cost? If you consider life insurance as an investment, is it really a good investment if you are guaranteed to lose for terminating the policy within 10 years or whenever your surrender period is? Even if you keep the policy past that period, the guaranteed growth rate is lower than the average securities market growth. Then you face another serious problem of fighting against inflation. I do believe in protecting what people have through insurance, but mixing insurance and investment is usually not a good idea. See an article from AARP.org (*Why Insurance and Investing Often Don't Mix*).

Who Can Benefit from Whole Life Insurance

I believe that people who can benefit most from whole life insurance are those who fully fund their qualified retirement accounts annually and are looking for ways to save more in tax-efficient ways. Individual life insurance premiums are not tax deductible, as opposed to retirement savings that can be deducted. But the money inside of a life insurance policy can grow tax-deferred, and death benefits are generally tax-free. That makes whole life insurance a good vehicle to inherit wealth in estate planning, but for most people who are not wealthy, the costs in whole life insurance and inability to deduct premiums seem to outweigh benefits of guarantees and fancy features of insurance. Buying a simple and inexpensive term life policy and maximizing the savings in tax-advantaged qualified retirement accounts is a better financial strategy for them. If you already have whole life insurance, consult a fee-only financial planner to discuss if keeping it makes sense. Fee-only (not fee-based) financial planners don't receive a commission from what they recommend, providing a better chance of unbiased advice.

Universal / Variable Life

Universal Life Insurance (UL)

Flexible Premiums + Potential Growth

As previously explained, premiums in whole life insurance do not change during the contract, but universal life, another permanent life insurance, allows flexible premium payments. When you buy universal life insurance, your policy is given a guaranteed minimum interest rate and a potential for higher returns. If the insurance company has a higher profit than expected, you may be given an excess interest amount. Based on the cash value, you can increase or decrease the premium payments within limits, as you need. Unlike whole life insurance that has a fixed death benefit, universal life policies *can* have a higher death benefit amount, depending on the cash value. The other side of the flexible premium feature is that you will have to pay higher premiums if your cash value is below the required minimum amount. See an article from Forbes.com warning about this potential problem (*Retirement Disaster Looms For Universal Life Policyholders*).

Variable Life Insurance (VL)

Investment Management

The main feature with variable life insurance is that policyholders can manage their investment. Variable life is another permanent life insurance for people who also want to have control over investment. Just like any securities investment, there's no guaranteed protection on principal with variable life insurance, which means you can lose money in it. Your premium, less fees and expenses, is separated from the general account into sub-accounts and managed by you. Because a portion of your premium is paid for the death benefit, there's a guaranteed minimum death benefit. The rest of your account value will be determined by your investment performance. Premiums are fixed throughout the policy contract.

Variable Universal Life Insurance (VUL)

Premium Flexibility + Investment Control

Variable universal life (VUL) insurance is a hybrid product between variable life and universal life insurance. Premium flexibility from universal life insurance and investment control from variable life insurance are the two dominant features in variable universal insurance. When your investment performs well, you can reduce the payment or even skip it, assuming enough cash value. If the opposite happens, your cash value will decrease, and you can be required to pay higher premiums.

Fancy Features Cost You Money

Like any other products, more features in insurance products generally come at higher costs. Universal life (UL) is permanent life insurance with premium flexibilities and a potential to get a higher interest rate than promised. Variable life (VL) is also permanent life insurance with investment control. Variable universal life (VUL) insurance is a combination of both: flexibility of premiums and control of investment. Sounds good, doesn't it? They all come with costs. You can be asked to pay higher premiums in universal life, and you can lose a large part of your investment in variable life insurance. A combination of both is possible for variable universal life insurance. Complex financial products tend to pay higher compensation to salespeople than simpler ones do, so agents are motivated to sell those with a higher commission and often emphasize 'great features' to prospects, ignoring costs and potential downsides. If you want to buy any permanent life insurance product, I highly recommend consulting a fee-only financial planner who doesn't sell insurance for a commission.

Annuity

Insurance Product for Retirement Income

Annuities are insurance products for individual retirement income. They are different from Social Security, which is a national pension program that is run by the federal government and funded with payroll taxes. The main difference between life insurance and an annuity is that life insurance is most beneficial to survivors in case of the insured's premature death, while annuity will benefit the annuitant (the person whose life an annuity is based on) the most in case of longevity. If I buy life insurance, my primary goal would be to financially protect my surviving family members in case of my premature death. If I purchase an annuity, my goal would be to protect myself from outliving my money with a continuous income stream.

Many Choices

People can buy an annuity and make payments or buy with lump sum cash and let it grow until retirement. If you don't take income right away, it is called a deferred annuity because you defer the benefits for a later time, usually until retirement. If you buy an annuity policy with your assets in 401(k) or Traditional IRA upon retirement and start taking payments immediately, it is called an immediate annuity.

Fixed annuities pay fixed interest rates and fixed benefits, while variable annuities are tied to investment performance with variable benefit payments. Because variable insurance products are involved in securities investment, agents who sell them must hold a securities license such as Series 7 and 66.

An equity-indexed annuity (EIA) is somewhat in the middle of variable annuity and fixed annuity: EIAs offer protection of principal and a minimum guarantee on return. The guaranteed return is minimal, but EIAs offer a potentially higher return, although it is capped. If the cap is 5% on an EIA and the benchmark index grows 10%, then the annuity account will earn 5%. If the market goes down, however, the annuity will make the minimum guaranteed return. Sounds good since you cannot lose, right? But EIAs are complex insurance products with higher surrender charges, causing higher overall costs to own than fixed annuities. Typical EIAs yield somewhat between fixed and variable annuities. Since EIAs are considered fixed annuities, insurance agents without securities licenses can sell them.

For annuity payout options, policyholders can decide if they want to get payments during one person's lifetime or both spouses'. An inflation rider, which increases the dollar amount of regular payments based on inflation, can also be purchased, which will lower initial benefit payments. A policyholder can have the remaining asset to pass onto his/her children, in case of death within a specified period such as 10 years from annuitization (time you convert your accumulated assets into an income stream). All attractive options cost money, of course. Think about it. What would cost an insurance company more: to sell a policy that guarantees to pay monthly benefit until both couples die or until just one of them dies? How about a policy that increases benefit payments to keep up with inflation or one with a fixed benefit that never increases? The first choice in both questions is better for policyholders and will cost more for insurance companies to provide, which is why an annuity with more attractive features usually pays lower monthly benefits.

Inflation Risk on Fixed Income

Many people prefer a fixed annuity for its simplicity and predictability, but I must point out, again, how those very features can hurt them, financially speaking. Remember the previous example of a $500,000 life insurance policy that in about 40 years would be worth significantly less due to inflation? Fixed annuities have the same purchasing power loss problem. You may think $2,000 monthly annuity income is good enough for now, for example, but if it doesn't increase with time, you'd soon find it not enough when prices of goods and services go up. You can buy an inflation protection rider, and then your initial payments will be less than $2,000. Consider this when you contemplate buying an annuity.

Taxation

Like other individual life insurance, the premiums paid on an annuity contract is not tax deductible, but the money can grow tax-deferred until withdrawals. Because the premiums were not tax-deductible at the time of the contribution, only the profits are taxed for distributions. For example, let's say you pay $100,000 into your annuity and it grows to $200,000 at the time of annuitization. Of the $200,000, 50% is your principal that was taxed already, and the other 50% is profit that has not been taxed. If you receive $10,000 this year from the annuity, half of the money, which is $5,000, is subject to ordinary income tax. However, if you buy an annuity with money from an account that has never been taxed on either principal or profits, such as 401(k) or Traditional IRA, then all distributions are taxable.

Penalty for Early Distributions

Because annuities are financial products that are designed for retirement income and monies can grow tax-deferred, there's a penalty for early withdrawals. If non-qualified distributions are made before age 59 ½, a penalty of 10% will be imposed on top of income taxes on profits, but not the principal, which is post-tax. This penalty may be waived under some conditions such as premature death, disability, medical expenses, etc. See more information on this subject on IRS.gov (*Topic 558 -*

Additional Tax on Early Distributions from Retirement Plans Other Than IRAs).

Shop Around

It is often said that 'annuities are sold, not purchased.' The infamous reputation was earned due to the complexity of annuity products and people who buy an annuity often don't fully understand the costs and the details of what they buy. A regular income stream until death can provide you great peace of mind, which is the main reason you may consider an annuity in retirement planning, but it is essential that you fully understand what you buy and evaluate if the costs are worth the potential benefits. If you want to buy an annuity, please shop around. Also consider no-load annuities, as they tend to have lower fees and some may even allow cancellation without penalty if you were to change your mind later. If you're not sure how you can evaluate annuities, or you flat out wonder if you *need* one, consult a financial planner who doesn't sell products.

Health Insurance

US Health Insurance System Is Complex

The American health insurance system is very complex. Medicare, which is for senior citizens 65 and older, is funded by workers through payroll taxes and run by the federal government. Medicaid, which is for people with low income regardless of age, is funded by the state and federal governments, but it is managed by states. While they mostly follow federal guidelines, each state can decide the eligibility and benefits of Medicaid. Military personnel and their families have their own health care system. Civilian government employees may have different health insurance and benefits. Employees of other organizations get health insurance through work if one is offered. People who are not offered group insurance get coverage on HealthCare.gov that was established by The Affordable Care Act (ACA), also known as Obamacare. The HealthCare.gov is a marketplace that is set up by the government for individuals to buy health insurance from private insurance companies. All plans offered in the exchange must follow ACA guidelines, and the federal government provides financial assistance to individuals based on their income. After all these, 12.2% of Americans are still uninsured as of the fourth quarter of 2017, according to Gallup (*U.S. Uninsured Rate Steady at 12.2% in Fourth Quarter of 2017*).

Costs

Health care spending in the US is the highest in the world, according to CNBC.com (*US Health-care Spending is High. Results are...Not So Good*). The average work-based health insurance premiums are $6,435 for single people and $18,142 for family in 2016, according to CNN.com (*Workers' Health Insurance Premiums Rise Modestly, but Deductibles Jump a Lot More*). That is $536 for singles and $1,512 for families per month!

As if the high insurance premiums are not enough, individuals often have to pay a lot of money before insurance companies start paying. Copay, deductible, co-insurance, and out-of-pocket maximum in health insurance dictate what amount and percentage of total costs patients are expected to pay. The higher those numbers, the lower monthly premium in general.

As I previously stated, about three-fourths of Americans live paycheck-to-paycheck with little or no savings. If you have income and don't have insurance, you have to pay a hefty penalty when you file your taxes, although that is to be eliminated in 2019. To avoid a penalty and minimize health insurance premiums, many people choose a policy with a high copay, high deductible, high percentage co-insurance, and high out-of-pocket maximum amount. When people have such insurance, they end up paying for most of their medical costs out of pocket. Thus, what naturally happens is that too many people forgo regular checkups and preventive care out of fear for what they may have to pay. For those who can afford it, traveling to a foreign country for medical procedures is rather common because it is cheaper even with international travel expenses. I know many people who visit Korea for checkups, surgeries, and other medical procedures even though they have health insurance in America. They say that it is often cheaper to go abroad for many medical tests and treatments without insurance.

Some of the many reasons for high medical costs in America are as followed: high administrative costs (more than double the average of OECD nations), defensive medicine (doctors order unnecessary multiple tests to avoid potential lawsuits), and lack of government negotiation power (it doesn't have legal authority to negotiate to lower drug costs for Medicare Part D, for example). Also, there's no standard pricing, so the price for the same medical treatment or test can be vastly different depending on where one gets it.

Regardless of who and what to blame for the high health care costs in America, it is imperative for individuals to understand the health care system to protect their finances. Know what your health insurance does and does not cover and understand terms.

Important Terms

Network

Doctors and health care providers can decide which insurance they accept by agreeing to discounted prices for services. If you use a doctor or a facility that is out of your insurance network, you may have to pay all or a significant portion of the costs out of pocket. Be sure to use service providers in your network, if possible. You can call your insurance company or health care providers to find who's in your network. Do not solely depend on the providers' websites since they may not be updated promptly.

Preventive Care Services

Per the Affordable Care Act of 2010, health insurance companies now provide annual basic preventive care services free of charge to insured members. Some of the services are blood pressure screening, cholesterol screening, depression screening, colorectal cancer screening, and immunization vaccines. The service items are different for adult men, adult women, and children. See Health care.gov for the list of preventive care services that you can get for free each year. (*Preventive Health Services*) Some insurance companies provide extra preventive care services, so know what they are and take advantage of them. But understand that health insurance plans that are sold outside of ACA may not offer such service.

Copayment

Copayment is a set amount that you pay every time you see a doctor or receive medical service, except for annual preventive care services. The amount varies depending on insurance plans and services. For example, it may cost you $25 to see your primary doctor, $35 for a specialist, and $200 for an emergency room visit. You may also have different copayments for prescription drugs depending on if they are generic or name brands.

Deductible

A deductible is a set amount, usually in thousands of dollars that a policyholder has to pay for services. The higher the deductible, the lower the insurance premiums, generally speaking. The average family deductible for 2017 on ACA is over $8,000 (eHealthInsurance.com). If you have an $8,000 deductible on your health insurance, it means that you could pay up to that amount in any given year before your insurance company pays for your medical service. Say you have a small surgery that is $5,000, then you could pay the full amount. If the operation was $10,000, then you could pay up to $8,000, and the insurance company would pay the remaining $2,000.

Coinsurance

Coinsurance is another way that you could pay before your insurance company pays. It is described as a proportional percentage such as 80/20 or 90/10 and is applied after deductible. Let's say that you have health insurance with a $5,000 deductible and 80/20 coinsurance. If you have a surgery that is $10,000, then your deductible of $5,000 would apply first, and the remaining $5,000 would be split between you and the insurance company. Since your coinsurance is 80/20, your insurance company would pay 80% of the remaining balance or $4,000 and the other 20%, $1,000, is your responsibility. In this scenario of your $10,000 surgery, your insurance company could only pay $4,000, while you're responsible for $6,000.

Out-of-Pocket Maximum

Your financial responsibility can increase further if you have a high out-of-pocket maximum. It is the maximum amount that you can expect to pay for medical costs in any given year. Let's say that your out-of-pocket maximum is $15,000, and you had a $100,000 surgery this year. Then you could pay up to $15,000 for copayment, deductible, and coinsurance, and your insurance company would pay the rest. By the way, this number resets each year, and you'd have to pay up to $15,000 if you were to have another procedure next year in this case. This is why so many people even with health insurance forgo non-life threatening medical services in America.

Qualifying Events

You can generally make changes to your health insurance only during an open enrollment period, which is usually a few months each year, but some situations, called qualifying events, will allow you to make changes outside of the limited duration. For example, if you lose your job (therefore lose health insurance as well), have a new baby, lose a family member from death or divorce, etc., then you can make a change on your coverage at any time. See *Qualifying Life Events (QLE)* on HealthCare.gov for more information on this subject.

One Procedure, Several Bills

What makes this already complex health care system even more so is how medical providers bill their patients. With one surgery, it is common for patients to get separate bills from the facility, testing labs, and all the doctors who are involved in the process. If you first see a specialist and she recommends a surgery, for example, she will send you a bill, the surgeon who performs the operation will bill you, and the anesthesiologist (if one is used) will also send you a separate bill, not to mention the facility in which the operation took place. If there are labs that some testing samples are sent to, you'll get bills from them, too. It is crucial that you understand what each bill is for and simultaneously deal with all the billers.

Checking Bills and Negotiating

One good thing from this complexity is that you *can* negotiate with the billers (though I would much rather be in a situation where people don't have to "negotiate" over medical bills). Depending on your circumstances, you may be able to get a big discount on your medical bills. It can be time-consuming to deal with all the billers, but it may well be worth your time. To do that, you need to know the details of charges, so first ask for an itemized bill from each service provider. Medical billing errors are known to be very common, hence, go through each charge to make sure that you received the service or item, and check if the dates of service and the number of items are correct, etc. If you don't understand what some of the charges are for, don't hesitate to ask the biller to explain. See this article, *How to Spot 8 Common Medical Billing Errors* on NerdWallet.com.

Chapter 4 | INSURANCE

It can be very difficult, if not impossible, to confirm the charges if you don't remember receiving services or treatments. It is best if you (or someone) can write down all the items and services as you receive them, including nominal items such as a box of tissue and a pair of sucks. Even for the same medical service, the billing rate can be different based on who conducts it (doctor vs. nurse, for example), so write down names and the position, too. Don't hesitate to ask the caregivers questions so you can correctly document what you are receiving. You can tell them why you are doing it, and even ask them to write for you if needed. Be very polite at all times. If billing errors are found, have the biller correct them and resubmit the claim to your insurance company. Don't expect your insurance company to proactively work with you on reducing charges because they usually have preset prices that they pay for each service. In other words, it almost doesn't matter to the insurance companies how much hospitals and doctors charge for a specific service because what the insurance company pays may remain the same. It saddens me to say this, but we are basically on our own when it comes to dealing with medical billing.

Once you finish correcting errors, be ready to explain to the billers, in writing, why those bills are such a financial burden on you and provide evidence when asked. Most medical facilities have a way to check your assets and liabilities, including your credit card limits. I've seen a hospital billing staff asking a patient to pay bills with a credit card. Do not allow that, as it is almost a sure way to your financial ruin. Nobody can force you to pay your medical bills on a credit card. Visit the local billing office(s), if possible, to negotiate in person. This article, *7 Smart Ways to Negotiate Your Medical Bills* on CNNMoney.com, may help.

Once you agree to payment arrangements, be sure to follow through. Don't be late, and if you face further financial hardship, be proactive and try to renegotiate.

Medical bills are the most significant cause for personal bankruptcies in the US, according to CNBC.com (*Medical Bills Are The Biggest Cause of US Bankruptcies*). Take medical debt seriously and don't let it ruin your finances. If you feel overwhelmed or cannot find time to manage it all, consider hiring a professional who can negotiate the medical debt for you. These services typically cost you about 20-30% of the savings that they get for you. For example, if a company can slash your $10,000 medical bill by 50%, then you'd pay $1,000-$1,500 (20-30% of $5,000 that was saved on your behalf) for their fee. Try to select a service provider carefully by reviewing what others say and avoid paying any upfront fees. If medical bills are suffocating your finance, consult a bankruptcy lawyer. I strongly discourage taking an early distribution from your retirement accounts to pay medical bills, as retirement assets *are* protected from garnishment for unpaid medical debt.

Utilize HSA

Health savings accounts (HSA) were created to help people with health care costs in the early 2000's. HSAs are like retirement accounts with excellent tax benefits and asset protection from most creditors, but better. It is better because distributions for qualified medical expenses are tax-free, as opposed to withdrawals from pre-tax retirement accounts that are all subject to taxation at distribution. Unlike pre-tax retirement assets that require minimum distribution once account owners turn 70 ½, HSAs don't have such distribution requirements. These features with HSAs are so attractive that they even make a good retirement strategy, which is why I further discuss HSAs in the later chapter for retirement planning.

The basic eligibilities to open an HSA is that one must have a high deductible health plan (HDHP) with a minimum of $1,350 ($2,700 for a family plan), yet maximum out-of-pocket should be no more than $6,650 ($13,300 for family). The maximum contribution amount is $3,450 for single and $6,900 for family ($3,500 or $7,000 in 2019). People who are 55 or older can save an extra $1,000, but they can no longer contribute once becoming eligible for Medicare at age 65.

Medicaid

As stated earlier, Medicaid is medical insurance for individuals with low income, regardless of age, and is funded by both federal and state governments. It also provides insurance to people with disabilities and pregnant women. The Medicaid program for children is called CHIP (Children's Health Insurance Program) and can be applied for separately from parents' insurance.

Since states manage Medicaid, each state can set its own rules on eligibility of who can qualify and with different income levels. Income levels to be eligible for children, adults, and pregnant women are usually different. Visit Medicaid.gov for your state's income levels for edibility (*Medicaid and CHIP Eligibility Levels*). As you would see on the website, states' eligibility is based on Federal Poverty Level (FPL) in most cases. For the year 2018, Federal Poverty Level (FPL) is $12,140 for individuals, $16,460 for a family of two, and $25,100 for a family of four.

Let's use a simplified example of income eligibility for Medicaid. Say you are a family of four living in Oklahoma, which requires an income of less than 205% of $25,100 FPL for CHIP and 41% for adults. If your family income is $50,000, your children under 18 are eligible for Medicaid in your state because your family income is less than $50,430 (205% of $24,600 FPL for a family of four). However, you, an adult who is not pregnant, are not eligible because your income must be less than $10,086 (41% of $24,600 FPL for a family of four) to be eligible. For that reason, it is not unusual that children are under Medicaid (CHIP) while adult members in the same household have separate health insurance coverage from ACA (Obamacare). States may also impose limits on amounts of assets one can own to be eligible for Medicaid and provide discounts based on other facts. Visit your local social service office or website for more information and to find out your (your children's) eligibility for Medicaid.

Medicare

Eligibility

People at age 65 can get Medicare, a national health care insurance for senior citizens. To be qualified for Medicare, one must have earned enough Social Security credits by paying into the system for a minimum of 10 years and be either a US citizen or permanent resident. Younger people with permanent disability or dialysis can also get Medicare. Spouses who haven't worked (paid into the system) can get Medicare based on their spouse's work history.

Ex-spouses of eligible workers can also join Medicare at 65 if they are single at the time of application and the marriage lasted over 10 years.

There are other conditions for Medicare eligibility: visit Medicare.gov to check if you are eligible (*Determine Your Eligibility or Calculate Your Premium*). Senior citizens who don't qualify for Medicare due to lack of work history can purchase Part A (covers costs for hospitals) for $232-$422 a month, depending on their income (2018).

Original Medicare vs. Medicare Advantage Plan

When it comes to Medicare, people have two options: Original Medicare (Part A and B) and Medicare Advantage Plan (Part C). Original Medicare is run by the federal government, while Medicare Advantage Plans are regulated by the federal government but provided by private insurance companies. Part A (which covers hospitals) is free for those who qualify, but Part B (which covers doctors and tests) is optional and has to be purchased. The monthly premium for Part B in 2018 is between $134-$268, depending on one's income. Unless you opt out of Medicare altogether because you have health insurance from your job or your spouse's, late enrollment for Part B can be penalized for life with higher premiums. Part D, which is for prescription drugs, is also optional, but a penalty applies for late sign-up. So it's recommended to sign up for Part B and D during the initial Part A enrollment period. Monthly premiums for Medicare Part D widely vary depending on your plan, what you need, and your income. Medicare Part B and D premiums are taken out of one's Social Security check. Vision and dental services are not generally covered in Original Medicare, and separate coverage must be purchased. Visit Medicare.gov for more cost-related information, including deductible and coinsurance (*Medicare 2018 Costs at a Glance*).

For simplicity and choices, many seniors consider Medicare Advantage plans. If you decide to buy Part C, instead of Part A & B, from a private insurer, then Medicare pays a certain amount to the insurance company on your behalf each month. Depending on options you choose, you'll pay the difference in premiums. Prices for Part C plans can widely vary, depending on what you want and where you live. Most Medicare Advantage plans come with prescription drugs (Part D) and other options that are not included in Original Medicare such as vision and dental coverage.

One significance of Original Medicare is that it does not have an out-of-pocket maximum, as opposed to Medicare Advantage plans that do. It means that you can burn through your life savings quickly if your health requires expensive medical service in the future. Carefully compare the two options, Original Medicare and Medicare Advantage plans, that are available in your state before making your choice. You can switch between the two during the regular enrollment period each year.

Enrollment

- *If you are 65 and already receiving Social Security benefits:* You'd be automatically enrolled for Original Medicare (Part A and B) and will get a Medicare card during the three months in the mail before your 65th birthday.
- *If you are 65 but not receiving Social Security benefits:* You need to sign up during the three months before and three months after your 65th birthday month. For example, if you turn 65 in July of this year, then you can apply for Medicare between April and October.
- *If you are under 65 and receiving Social Security benefits due to disability:* You would be automatically enrolled for Original Medicare (Part A and B) and receive a card before the 25th month of receiving SS disability benefits.

- *If you are over 65, not receiving SS benefit, and missed the enrollment period:* You can sign up during the general enrollment period, which is January 1st through March 31st. You may have to pay a higher premium for your policy because of late enrollment.
- *If you are over 65, not receiving SS benefits, and opted out for Medicare because you had group health insurance through work:* You can sign up for Medicare without penalty during the special enrollment period once you leave work (therefore lose health insurance).
- *If you need to change your policy:* You can make changes to your plan during the general enrollment period, which is January 1st through March 31st.

Medicare Supplement Insurance Policies

Original Medicare has a copay, deductible, and coinsurance, but as previously explained, it does not have an out-of-pocket maximum, which means there is no limit that one can pay for medical expenses. Those who have Original Medicare (Part A and B) and want to protect their retirement assets by putting a gap in what they have to pay for medical expenses can purchase an extra policy, called Medigap. People with a Part C plan cannot buy Medigap. There are 10 standardized policies in Medigap (A, B, C, D, F, G, K, L, M, and N), and they are regulated by the federal government (2018). Private insurance companies sell these plans and depending on where you live, some plans may not be available. Prices and benefits for these plans also vary, so one must understand what plan he or she needs and carefully compare prices before purchasing. See *How to Compare Medigap Policies* on Medicare.gov.

Politics

When it comes to retirement and health care, politics affect individuals and their money significantly. The number one reason for personal bankruptcies in America is due to medical debts. You may be young and healthy now, thinking you don't need to worry about that yet, but everybody gets old and will eventually need health care service. The policies you support today will affect your medical benefits (and costs) later in your life, not to mention they may be currently affecting your loved ones.

Insurance companies exist to make money. If it is up to them, they would not provide coverage to people with pre-existing conditions, kick sick people out of insurance once the cost of benefits paid is more than premiums received, charge very high premiums to old or sick people, and limit maximum lifetime benefits. Well, that is actually what insurance companies used to do until ACA (Obamacare) was enacted, although these rules seem to be weakening under President Trump who promised to abolish ACA and got elected

I support a free market, but there are areas in which a free market just cannot work, the health insurance system being one of them. Think about it. Companies cannot exist if they don't make money. How will insurance companies make money by providing quality benefits to sick and old people? Without young and healthy people or the government subsidizing the costs, it is mathematically impossible for a private company to run a health insurance system that is affordable. I honestly don't see how we can fix our health care problem without a national system like Social Security or Medicare that mandates all workers to pay.

Regardless, we can argue what a good health insurance system is, and how we can pay for it. To have a constructive debate on this grave issue, we must first understand how policies that we support affect us. If you don't want the government to impose much regulation in the health care industry, for example, then realize your insurance company may kick you out when you need it most. If you are one of those who are covered by "good" insurance through the government, remember that other taxpayers are likely subsidizing your benefits. I hope you're sympathetic of those who are paying for your benefits but cannot afford the same for themselves. More importantly, without constraining ever-increasing medical costs or tax increase, your "good" health insurance benefits are likely to be reduced. Don't assume you won't ever need to buy individual insurance because you are currently covered by your employer plan. You will lose your health insurance if you get sick and cannot work anymore.

My point is that everything is correlated. Every health care policy has financial consequences, and we *all* pay one way or another. Understand what health care policies that you support mean to you and others. When you're supporting a policy that'll take other people's benefits away, remember that you or your loved ones may end up needing the same care someday. In that sense, we all are in the same boat with a leaking floor. If you are on the top floor, you may not think the danger is imminent to your safety and are less motivated to help those in trouble, but if you don't help them as if that is your problem, the water will eventually get you, too. Please understand that your health and money *are* significantly affected by policies and politicians. Ignore anyone who tells you not to be political, and get out and *vote*. Unless you are very wealthy, we all are just one sickness away from financial ruin.

Auto Insurance

Mandatory in Most US States

It is illegal to drive without auto insurance in most states in the US. In a few states that do not require auto insurance, drivers must prove financial ability to pay in case of an accident. Consider auto insurance a necessary cost of driving and owning a car.

Liability vs. Comprehensive Policy

People can buy either liability only or comprehensive (full) policy. Liability insurance covers damage you cause to other people and their property. It is cheaper than comprehensive insurance, and it is the minimum insurance most states require from drivers. It may make sense to have just liability insurance if you drive a car with low salvage value. If you decide to get only liability insurance, be sure to have emergency funds saved to repair your damage or buy a new car, in case of an accident that is your fault. Comprehensive (full) insurance covers all damages that you cause both on the other party's property and on yours. It also covers loss from theft and weather damage on your automobile. It is, of course, more expensive than liability only.

Auto Insurance Terms

Bodily Injury Liability: Covers damages caused to people in case of an accident at your fault. It covers loss of wage, medical expenses, and pain and suffering. If you have a $50,000/$100,000 coverage, it means that your insurance will pay up to $50,000 per person and up to a total of $100,000 per accident.

Property Damage Liability: Covers damages caused by you to property such as a car, fence, tree, etc.

Uninsured or Underinsured Motorists: Although this is often a part of liability insurance that states require, it benefits you. It will pay you for any damage that was caused by a driver who does not have insurance or have insurance that is not enough to cover the full damage.

Collision: Pays for the damage on your car in case of a collision with an object such as another vehicle, fence, tree, etc. Your deductible applies to this coverage. Let's say you run into a tree and the damage on your vehicle is worth $2,000. If your deductible is $500, then your insurance will pay the cost minus your deductible, which is $1,500 ($2,000-$500).

Comprehensive: Covers damages on your car caused by other than collision, such as from theft, fire, animal, hail, flood, etc. Deductible applies to this coverage, too.

Medical Payment: Covers medical costs for you and your passengers. This amount is relatively low in general compared to other coverage because you can use your health insurance for most medical expenses.

Rental: If you need a rental car while your car is being repaired, this coverage will pay a limited amount for the rental costs. It is determined per day, and there's a maximum. If it is $30/$1,000, for instance, the insurance company will pay up to $30 per day and a total of $1,000 per accident on a rental car.

Road Service: This pays for road emergency such as delivering gas and towing to a repair shop.

What Affects Auto Insurance Premiums

Auto insurance premiums are affected by various things: type of car you drive, amount of coverage, how much you drive, previous claim(s), where you live/park, deductibles, your age, profession/education, credit score, etc. A non-moving violation such as illegal parking doesn't usually affect the insurance rate, but any moving violation such as speeding and improper turns can. Getting moving violation tickets can cost you both hefty fines and an increase in your auto insurance premium. So follow speed limits and obey street signs for the sake of your pocket as well as for your safety. Besides, accumulated points can even result in your license revocation. States have different point systems. See how your state's system works on DMV.org (*DMV Point System*).

Shop Around

Shop around to get a better quote. Thanks to the Internet, you can now quickly check quotes online, and some companies even show competitors' prices as well. Take advantage of all eligible discounts. For example, you may be able to get a discount if you are a member of the military, bundle insurance, have good grades as a student, have a security system in your vehicle, etc.

Be sure to get enough coverage and the deductible that you can afford. If you don't have enough insurance to cover the damage you cause, you can be personally sued. If you don't have enough savings to cover your deductible amount, then you may not be able to fix the damage on your car. Carefully analyze what you need to protect your assets and what you can afford to be adequately insured.

Chapter 4 | INSURANCE

What to Do in Case of an Accident

Getting involved in an accident can cause anxiety, and you may forget what you are supposed to do in such a situation. I know someone who got hit by another motorist but immediately left the scene to go to work. He said that the accident impact made him dizzy and he couldn't think straight at that moment. He later realized what he did (didn't do) and reported the accident. Luckily for him, the person who hit him also reported to the police and her insurance paid for the damage on his car. If she had left the scene without reporting the accident, he would have had to pay for the damage that he didn't cause. Some recommendations that you should follow in a crash are:

- Remain calm
- Report the accident to the police
- Gather information such as names (including passengers), address, insurance, license, and auto information (make, year, model, etc.)
- Take photos of the damage and the scene
- Report to your insurance agent/company

For more information on what to do in case of an accident, visit NAIC.org (National Association of Insurance Commissioners).

Other Things to Consider

Auto insurance is for financial protection in case of unexpected events such as an accident. Too many claims to your insurance will result in a premium increase or rejection of coverage, so use it wisely. Pay for any damage that is equal to or less than your deductible out of your pocket. If, for example, you hit your (or someone else's) mailbox or garage door, the repair costs may be less than your deductible. Even if the cost is slightly more than your deductible, still consider paying it, especially if you had a previous claim in the last three to five years. It may not be worth reporting to your insurance, thus risking a rate increase, if you have to pay all or most of the costs in the name of deductible anyway.

Depending on your state and a court judge, you may be able to hire an attorney and "fix" a moving violation ticket to a non-moving violation one. You will have to pay the ticket price and court fees, on top of attorney fees, but it would not affect your auto insurance premium. If you get a moving violation ticket, see if it may be worth hiring an attorney to have it fixed to a non-moving violation ticket, assuming your state allows it.

Understand that if you use your vehicle for work other than commuting—delivering pizzas, for example—your auto insurance will not likely cover any damage that is caused during work activities. Your auto insurance is for personal use, and you need separate commercial auto insurance for that. Also, auto insurance generally follows the insured car. If you let your friend drive your car and he causes an accident, your insurance will have to pay for the damage, not your friend's insurance.

Homeowners Insurance

Not Required by Law, But by Lenders

Homeowners (HO) insurance is for protecting your property from unexpected losses. Unlike auto insurance that is required by states, you can own a house without homeowner's insurance if you don't have a mortgage. For homeowners with a mortgage, lenders will require home insurance. Even if you don't have any loan on your home and insurance is not required by anyone, you should have insurance, and the premiums should be considered as a part of the costs of home ownership.

What Is Not Covered

Let's start with what is *not* covered in homeowners (HO) insurance. Generally, homeowners insurance does not cover damages caused by movement of land and by uprising waters. For example, damages caused by wind and rains are covered, but damages caused by flood or earthquakes are usually not. If heavy rain and wind damage your roof and windows, your insurance will pay for the repair, minus your deductible. If the rain doesn't drain and causes flood damage in your basement, it won't be covered. If a large tree falls on your roof from heavy wind, the damage will be covered by your HO insurance, whereas if the tree falls because of an earthquake, it won't likely be covered. Damages that are caused by war, terrorism, or nuclear hazard are not generally covered, either, but you can buy extra coverage for earthquake, flood, and terrorism. Any damage that is caused intentionally by the homeowner is not covered.

HO Insurance Terms

Dwelling: Dwelling covers any loss on your home and attached structures such as your garage and deck. You should occasionally check the coverage to make sure that it is enough for potential repair or replacement costs, as they tend to increase over time. Have enough coverage to rebuild your home, but understand that you don't need to "protect" the land your house is sitting on because it won't likely to get damaged in case of fire or tornado, for example.

Other Structures: It covers detached structures such as a storage area on your backyard and a detached garage. The coverage limit is usually 10% of Dwelling. The insurance company will not pay for the loss if you run a business from other structures.

Personal Property: Your personal properties that you can take with you when you move such as electronics, furniture, appliances, paintings, etc. will be insured under this coverage. It is usually 50% of Dwelling. For example, if your Dwelling coverage is $300,000, then the coverage on personal properties would be about $150,000. One important thing that you should understand is that this coverage with most homeowners insurance pays for losses at actual cash value (ACV). ACV is the current value, not the purchase price. For example, say you bought a new TV for $3,000 three years ago, and it is worth $1,000 today. If you have a fire in your home and the TV gets damaged, your insurance company will pay only $1,000. If you have relatively new personal properties, I recommend you get insurance that pays losses based on the replacement cost (RC). In the example above, your insurance policy will pay $3,000 (assuming that is how much your TV still costs to buy today) under RC. The premium may be about 10-15% higher to have a replacement cost (RC) endorsement. Do your math to see if it makes sense to pay an extra premium. Finally, there are usually limits on personal property losses: $1,500 on jewelry and $250 on coin collections, for instance. If you have any personal property that is valuable or collectible, get an endorsement. You are likely to be asked to provide an appraisal for each item.

Loss of Use: It pays costs of housing, such as a hotel stay, while your house is being repaired. It also pays loss of income if you were renting out your home. The maximum coverage is usually limited to 20% of Dwelling.

Personal Liability: It covers the homeowner's liability that causes bodily injury and property damage to others. If someone gets injured in your property, this coverage will pay for the damage and lawsuit-related costs, if any. Most insurance starts with a $100,000 for personal liability coverage, but at least $300,000-$500,000 is recommended in general. If you are likely to have potential damage or loss in your property, consider a higher coverage. Some examples of possible damage or loss would be if you have pets that can hurt people or if you have a pool and often invite other people to swim. If you have more assets to protect than what your homeowner's insurance pays for in personal liability, consider an umbrella policy (explained later).

Medical Payment: This is coverage for others who are injured on your property, whether or not it is your fault. It does not pay for the medical expenses of the homeowners and household members.

Deductible: This is the amount that you pay before the insurance company pays for the claimed damage. Like auto and health insurance, the higher the deductible, the less premium you pay in general. Don't choose a deductible that you cannot afford. For example, if you have $2,000 in emergency funds, then your deductible should not be higher than.

Things to Consider

First, lying can bite you hard, so don't lie with your insurance application. There are many things that affect homeowners insurance premiums such as smoke alarms, a pool, pets, age of roof, smoking, security system, etc. Intentional misstatement may be able to lower your premiums for now, but when you need the insurance most, your claim can be denied based on that. Being a few years off on the age of your roof may be an honest mistake that will not reject your claim, but stating that you don't smoke inside of the house when you occasionally do or saying that you have an alarm system when you don't, is a lie and can cause your claim to be denied.

Second, take good care of your property and keep good records. If you purchase new appliances or install a new roof, for example, save the papers. And make a list of your personal property items in your home with receipts and photos. Write down not only big items and recent purchases but also small personal items such as clothes, tools, dishes, hobby related things, books, etc. Doing so will help you include all the items you lost and make your claim process smoother. See if it may cost more for you to replace all the things on your list than the personal property coverage amount on your insurance. If so, consider a higher coverage.

Finally, shop around regularly. Insurance companies raise insurance premiums based on their data. Even if you never file any claim, your premium can still significantly increase if people in your area have many claims through the same company. That is why it is a good idea to check with different companies occasionally. You often, but not always, can save money by purchasing auto and home insurance from the same company. And make sure your policy has all the correct information about you and your property. Read the fine print on your policy to understand what may be excluded.

Other Insurance

Disability Insurance

Disability insurance is to supplement an insured's lost income caused by injury or sickness. The New York Times reports that the probability of a 20-something-year-old person becoming disabled (unable to go to work for at least several months because of injury or sickness) before retirement age is close to 30% *(Life and Disability Insurance)*. Social Security provides disability income (SSDI). However, with the average monthly disability benefit of around $1,200 per month and the average approval processing time of about a year, SSDI does not provide much financial comfort for most people to rely on, yet disability insurance is not as wildly discussed or purchased as it should be. That is mainly because premiums can be quite expensive, greatly varying depending on one's age, occupation, health condition, necessary income, etc. Providing insurance products with such high probability of losses is too risky for insurance companies, therefore needing to charge premiums that most people cannot afford. It is generally cheaper if purchased as a group, so if your company offers one, take advantage of it. When money is tight, you should prioritize retirement savings above disability insurance, in my opinion, because the probability of your retirement at some point is almost 100%, which is much higher than the chance of you becoming disabled. Regardless, when considering individual disability insurance, shop around and read the fine print.

Long-Term Care Insurance

We all get old and are highly likely to need help someday with daily activities such as eating, clothing, and using the bathroom. The problem is that those are expensive in-person services. According to AARP, the average annual nursing home cost is over $50,000 and rising fast (*Nursing Homes: Cost and Coverage*). The price can vary widely, depending on the area you live. I recently visited a family member at a nursing home in St. Louis, Missouri. The facility was nice, but not luxurious in any way. The area was not known for being expensive for locals, either. The nursing home price? Over $10,000 a month! Health insurance, whether it is private or group insurance from work, usually doesn't pay for a long-term care (LTC) facility like nursing homes. Medicare pays for a short-term stay. That is why living in a nursing home can quickly exhaust old and sick people's lifetime savings. AARP reports that only one-third of residents in nursing homes in the US are paying from their savings. Costs for the other two-thirds are paid by Medicaid, a government-run health care system for individuals with low income. Medicaid eligibility depends on each state, and it will only pay for nursing home facilities that are approved by the program, whose quality and location you may or may not like.

What can you do, then, if you want to protect your assets? You can purchase long-term care (LTC) insurance. Like disability insurance, group LTC insurance usually provides better rates. So take advantage of it if you are offered one through work or other membership. If you buy one individually, rates vary by your circumstances such as age, health condition, amount of coverage, term, etc.

Insurance companies are there to make money and will try to filter out conditions that may cause them to lower their profits. For example, if you have a pre-existing condition, it may be excluded for benefit purposes. Maximum benefits may be limited as well, for example, $150 per day for 10 years. Also, you should consider inflation when purchasing any insurance for a fixed future benefit. You may think $300 per day should be sufficient for today's nursing home costs, but it is not likely the case in 10 or 30 years when you need it. Nevertheless, there are many more things to consider before purchasing a long-term care policy. Read the following two articles: *Understanding Long-Term Care Insurance* on AARP.org and *10 Questions to Ask Before Buying Long-Term Care Insurance* on Forbes.com.

Umbrella Insurance

Umbrella insurance is extra insurance that pays for personal liability beyond auto and homeowners insurance liability coverage. For example, say your liability coverage on the auto insurance is $500,000, and you cause an accident with $1,000,000 damage. Your auto insurance company would pay $500,000, leaving the other $500,000 in damage unpaid. Then the person you cause the damage to would sue you for the difference. At this point, your personal assets such as cash, investments, and even your income can be garnished unless you have umbrella insurance. Umbrella insurance is designed to protect your personal liability in this kind of situation.

Umbrella insurance usually starts with a million dollars, and it is quite inexpensive at about $150-$350 per year. That is because it is an extra layer of protection and has strict conditions. You are required to have a certain amount of liability coverage on your auto and home insurance to qualify for an umbrella policy, usually at $500,000. Liabilities caused by activities with high risk such as car racing and boxing are likely to be excluded. Also, some companies may not even sell you one if you have young adults (age 14-22) or senior citizens over 85 years of age in your household. Shop around and find coverage that can protect you from potential liability. The coverage amount should be more than your total assets. Personal umbrella insurance does not cover liabilities caused by business-related activities, as business umbrella insurance needs to be purchased separately.

Business General Liability

As the name implies, it is for potential losses for your business. Depending on the type of your business entity, your liability from business activities can make your personal assets vulnerable to lawsuits. If a customer slips on your premise or gets sick or hurt from your products, for instance, he can sue you or your business for damage. Your general business liability insurance can cover such damage, up to the limit per your policy. If you have damage to your business from events that are covered such as a tornado or fire, your insurance can pay for the repair and lost income as well. Like home and auto insurance, premiums for this insurance can be affected by many things such as type of business and location, number of employees, amount of coverage, personal property such as machines needed for business, previous claims, other conditions, and deductibles etc. Make sure you are adequately covered, but also do not pay for what you don't need. Good record keeping of income and assets is vital for claims. Finally, continue to check prices occasionally to make sure you are not overpaying, and consider getting commercial umbrella insurance as well.

Workers Compensation Insurance

Commonly known as Workers' Comp, this insurance pays employees, including the owners, for damage and lost income from work-related injuries or sickness. It covers damage caused both on and off the business site, as long as the activities are work-related. If an employee was hurt during traveling, delivering, or attending a seminar for work, workers' compensation insurance will pay for the employee medical expenses and lost income while being treated.

Like other insurance products, each state regulates workers' compensation insurance and may mandate all businesses buy it. In Missouri, for instance, business owners who have more than five employees, whether they are part time or full time, are required to have this insurance. Even if your state exempts you from this insurance, it is still a good idea to buy it if you have any employee. Consider workers' compensation insurance as a part of running a business, along with general liability insurance. See *Worker's Compensation 101* on Entrepreneur.com for more information.

Chapter 5
RETIREMENT PLANNING

The national retirement picture is gloomy, as pension plans are disappearing and personal savings are lacking in this era in which the majority of people live paycheck-to-paycheck. Most retirees are living on Social Security that was designed to provide only one-third of post-retirement income. No matter how impossible it may seem, we must save today to prevent a gloomier future.

1. Retirement Problem in America
2. Why Retirement Accounts?
3. Individual Retirement Accounts
4. Group Retirement Plans
5. Social Security
6. Retirement Planning
7. Other Things to Consider

Chapter 5 | RETIREMENT PLANNING

Retirement Problem in America

I cannot stress enough how serious retirement problems are in America. I used to think that old people didn't buy new clothes because they didn't care about how they looked anymore. While some people may care less about their fashion as they get older, I now understand that their financial difficulties are more likely the reasons that they stop buying new clothes once retired. Getting a new jacket becomes a low priority when you struggle to pay for basic needs for surviving such as medicine and food. In this section, I'll further discuss how bleak America's retirement problems are, and why personal savings are critical, even if you have a "good" pension plan.

Lack of Savings

According to the 2015 report by US GAO (Government Accountability Office), 29% of Americans who are 55 or older do not have retirement saving or a pension plan (*Most Households Approaching Retirement Have Low Savings*). That means almost one in three people you and I know who are 55 or older are likely to have no savings or a pension plan. It becomes worse when we account for all Americans: CNN Money.com reports that 76% of Americans live paycheck-to-paycheck with little or no emergency savings (*76% of Americans are living paycheck-to-paycheck*). That is scary.

Disappearing Pension Plans

Pension plans (also called defined benefit plans or DB plans) pay specified amounts or a percentage of pre-retirement income until the retirees' (or the surviving spouse's) death. With a pension plan, employees don't have to do anything, other than working for their company. Employers, on the other hand, are responsible for the funding, management of assets, and the benefit payments in pension plans. Pension funds are commingled for all the beneficiaries, meaning employees don't have an individual account.

Increasing Costs of Pension Plans

Now, think about how people tend to live longer as technology and medicine advance. When the Social Security pension plan began after the Great Depression, an average worker was expected to live about 10 years after retiring at 65. But for those who retire at 65 today, women are expected to live for about 20 years and men for about 18 years. Longer lifespan directly increases organizations' financial liabilities for their pension plans. Most large companies that can afford pension plans are also publicly traded with shareholders pressuring the management to maximize profits. It is fiscally challenging, if not impossible, to keep paying the pension benefits that keep increasing. That is why the number of private sector workers who are covered by a pension plan rapidly decreased since the peak of 46% in 1980 (Employee Benefit Research Institute) to 8% in March of 2017 (Bureau of Labor Statistics).

Covered by a "Safe" Public Pension Plan?

If you are covered by a public pension plan, you may not think you need to worry about your retirement. Not so fast. Although most workers in the public sector are still covered by a pension plan, the future is not too promising for the same mathematical reasons. For their promised pension benefits to continuously be paid in the era of increasing longevity, either the pension trust funds must continue to grow significantly or taxes have to go up, simplistically speaking. I'll leave it up to you to decide how you would respond to a tax increase proposal to pay for government employees' retirement benefits. The economic growth all around the world, on the other hand, has been painfully slow in the past decade and expected to continue the trend. When the economy is bad where people lose jobs or income doesn't grow, taxes collected decrease. That puts enormous financial distress on governments to meet their financial obligations, including pension payments to their retirees. The bankruptcy filed by the city of Detroit, Michigan, in 2013, exemplifies what can happen to financially distressed municipalities. One of the big problems that Detroit had was due to pension benefit liabilities to its retirees, another one being health care costs.

Sadly, the problem is not unique to Detroit; it applies to the nation, including the federal government. An article on Forbes.com warns that "American governments are making promises that American taxpayers can't keep," therefore "massive future tax increases, substantial reduction of benefits, or some costly combination of the two" is inevitable (*A Solution to Our Public Pension Problem*). So whether you are covered by a federal or local government pension plan (soldier, judge, police officer, firefighter, civilian government employee, etc.) or a public school teacher pension plan, it is imperative to understand that your future retirement benefits may significantly decrease, and you should prepare for it while you can. Because of this fiscal problem with pension plans, the growing trend is that more and more public organizations are luring their employees into Social Security and a non-pension plan such as 403(b) and 401(k).

Issues with Salary Deferral Plans

With the decrease of pension plans, employee salary deferral plans (also called defined contribution –DC- plans) such as 401(k)s have gained popularity since the 1980's. It was the tipping era when the burden of retirement savings was largely transferred to employees from employers. As explained earlier, pension plans are funded and managed by employers, and employees don't have to do anything other than working hard for the company until retirement. But with 401(k) plans, employees are suddenly responsible for saving and managing their own retirement funds. Employers pay a small percentage of employees' payroll (typically 2-4%) into each participant's account, but even that may be optional, depending on the type of 401(k) plan they have. Employees now have to know how much they should save and make investment decisions. Other than Social Security pension benefits, retirees must live with whatever they saved for the rest of their lives.

While some people may thrive in this do-it-yourself system, the overwhelming majority is doomed to fail, in my view. To adequately prepare for retirement in this system, people need to understand how much they should save and how they can utilize tax benefits that are given to qualified retirement plans. They also need to know types of securities, how they are managed, and how fees are charged. Most people are not trained in these areas nor have interest or time to study them. Decreasing pension plans allowed companies to save money, and shareholders and top managers benefited from it. Shifting retirement funding and managing responsibilities to employees who were not ready, however, resulted in the desperate retirement problem we have today. It is almost like letting a child suddenly be in charge of the household finance without any training.

Social Security Problems

"How about Social Security?" you may ask. Well, we should not entirely rely on SS benefits for retirement income. Social Security was initially designed to provide about one-third of retirees' income with the other two-thirds being pension benefits and personal savings. As you know, pension plans are hard to find anymore, and most people cannot save while living paycheck-to-paycheck. Current average Social Security benefit payment is about $1,400 per month (January 2018). Moreover, Social Security funds are expected to be depleted by 2034 and benefits are to be reduced, unless the Congress acts to fix it. Don't worry, Social Security (SS) benefits won't just disappear in the near future as some people fear, but it sure needs help to keep the current level of benefits. And without any fix (which is likely to result in payroll tax increases), the benefit is expected to be reduced by about one-fourth around 2034. That means the average SS benefit would be worth about $1,000/mo. in today's value. Can you live on that?

Why Retirement Accounts?

The government is well aware of the retirement crisis, so it encourages people to save by providing incentives. The three most significant benefits are that the contributions can be deducted for income tax purposes, the money can grow tax-deferred until withdrawals, and the assets are protected from most creditors. I'll first explain tax benefits that can be categorized into two types, depending on contributions: pre-tax contributions and post-tax contributions.

Benefits on Pre-tax Contributions

How Deferring Taxes Can Help Asset Accumulation

All qualified retirement contributions are either pre-tax or post-tax. Contributions in a 401(k), Traditional IRA, SIMPLE IRA, and 403(b) account are pre-tax, meaning that the monies you save in those accounts are deductible for your income tax purposes. In a simplified example, let's say your overall income tax rate is 25%, and you save $10,000 in your 401(k) account this year. Then you'd be able to save about $2,500 in income taxes. Being able to 'defer' the income tax liability, allowing you to invest the total $10,000 can greatly help one's asset accumulation. This contribution deductibility feature is not allowed in regular brokerage accounts. If you want to save the same $10,000 in a non-retirement brokerage account, for example, then you'd first have to pay income taxes of $2,500 and can save only $7,500. Moreover, with a non-retirement brokerage account, you will also have to pay taxes on the gains each year, whereas with retirement accounts, you do not have to pay any taxes regardless of profits as long as the money is inside of the account. See the example below how $10,000 can result differently in 401(k) vs. non-retirement account after one year. A 7% return and 15% long-term (longer than one year) capital gains tax are used in this example.

Chapter 5 | RETIREMENT PLANNING

	401(k)	Non-ret. Acct.
Amount	$10,000	$10,000
Income tax 25%	0	-2,500
Actual saving	10,000	7,500
7% return	700	525
Capital gains tax 15%	0	-79
Balance after 1 year	$10,700	$7,946

Imagine how much difference the assets will be if one person keeps saving $10,000 pre-tax per year in a 401(k), while the other saves $7,500 after tax in a non-retirement account for a few decades? Take a look at the following table to see the difference over 10, 20, and 30 years.

	401(k)	Non-ret. Acct.
Balance after 10 years	$147,836	$104,492
Balance after 20 years	$438,652	$290,741
Balance after 30 years	$1,010,730	$622,715

Again, the reason that the person with a non-retirement account can save only $7,500 is that he has to pay an income tax of $2,500 first, while the person with a 401(k) account can *defer* the income tax and save the entire $10,000. Besides, the person with the non-retirement account has to pay capital gains taxes each year. It is a hypothetical example, and there can be many variables that can make differences: investment returns, personal income tax rate, fees, whether or not the investment in a non-retirement account has taxable gains, etc. The benefits of pre-tax savings and tax-deferral until distribution inarguably make a big difference in total assets over time. These great tax benefits are only available on qualified requirement accounts.

Snowball Effect of Tax Deferral and Employer Match

By the way, many companies offer a match of 2-4% of the employee's salary in their 401(k) plan. That means $1,400-$4,200 additional savings per year in your account, assuming $70,000 income. Can you imagine what the difference would be with that match? Let's see how that looks with 3.5% of the company match, or $2,450/yr. extra savings, shall we? Let's see what happens after 10, 20, and 30 years all in one table.

	401(k)	Non-ret. Acct.
Amount	$10,000	$10,000
Company match	2,450	0
Income tax 25%	0	-2,500
Actual saving	12,450	7,500
7% return	872	525
Capital gains tax 15%	0	-79
Balance After 1 Year	$13,322	$7,946
Balance after 10 years	$184,056	$104,492
Balance after 20 years	$546,121	$290,741
Balance after 30 years	$1,258,359	$622,715

Again, this is only a hypothetical example, but I hope you can see the "secret" for financial stability: taking full advantage of those tax benefits and employer match, if available.

Taxation

Chapter 5 | RETIREMENT PLANNING

One thing that I need to point out is tax implications with distributions from those pre-tax retirement accounts. Because no income taxes are paid on contributions *and* the profits, you need to pay taxes when you withdraw after retirement. If, for instance, you withdraw $20,000 from your pre-tax retirement account in a year after retirement, then you'll have to pay federal and state income taxes on that amount. It is likely that your income tax rate will be lower after retirement compared to now while you're working, but that is a future tax policy that we cannot foresee now.

You can withdraw (and pay income taxes) from your retirement accounts anytime after you turn 59 ½. An extra 10% penalty is imposed for early withdrawals made before age 59 ½, though there are some exceptions to the penalty (*Exceptions to Tax on Early Distributions - IRS.gov*). You can also keep the funds (and let the money continue to grow in the account) without paying any taxes until 70 ½. Once you turn 70 ½, however, you will have to withdraw minimal amounts (known as required minimum distribution or RMD). The RMD is there for the government to collect taxes that had been deferred for so long. See IRS.gov for more information on RMDs (*Required Minimum Distributions*). The penalty for not taking RMD is severe at an eye-popping 50%.

Benefits on Post-tax Contributions

Your contribution to a qualified retirement account is said to be post-tax or Roth when income taxes are paid first. In Roth accounts, you pay taxes before contribution, but you never pay taxes on qualified distributions. Besides, unlike pre-tax contributions where you have to take minimum distribution after 70 ½ and pay income taxes, you can keep Roth assets until you die. That is because there are no taxes to be paid. If you don't need to take any money out of your Roth account, then you can let the money keep growing as long as you are alive. For this reason, some wealthy people utilize Roth accounts in estate planning.

Another benefit of Roth accounts is that you can withdraw the principal any time without consequences. The reason behind this flexibility is because the income taxes are already paid before contributed into Roth accounts. Income taxes and 10% penalty will be imposed on profit withdrawals if the distribution is non-qualified. For example, you contributed a total of $30,000 in your Roth IRA and earned 20% ($6,000) profits over three years with the ending balance of $36,000. Early next year comes, and you, younger than 59 ½, withdraw $30,000. No tax problem exists because that is within the post-tax principal amount. However, if you withdraw the total amount of $36,000, then you'll have to pay income taxes and 10% penalty on the $6,000 profit.

Although this flexibility can be useful, I strongly discourage people from withdrawing money from their Roth accounts. That is because while you can freely withdraw principal amounts any time no matter how large, you cannot deposit them back because your annual contributions are limited. For a Roth IRA, the maximum contribution amount in 2018 is $5,500 ($6,500 if 50 or older). In the previous case, you *can* withdraw $30,000 principal for an emergency without any tax or penalty, but you can contribute only up to the annual limit. And besides, it is for your retirement savings, so consider them untouchable until you retire. See more explanation on Roth accounts in the following "Individual Retirement Accounts" section.

Protection from Creditors

Assets in qualified retirement accounts, regardless of whether they are pre-tax or post-tax contributions, are protected from most creditors. Employer-sponsored qualified retirement plan assets are protected with no limit, along with employee benefit plans such as FSA (Flexible Spending Account) and HSA (Health Savings Account). Individual retirement accounts such as IRAs and Solo 401(k) are subject to state regulations, and there may be a limit, although most states put exemptions over $1.2 million. Further, states may have different asset protection rules on Traditional vs. Roth IRAs.

That is a significant advantage when considering that other personal assets such as monies in bank accounts and other non-retirement accounts can be vulnerable to creditors. The legal protection on retirement assets applies even in case of bankruptcy. A few cases that your retirement accounts can be vulnerable are, but not limited to, alimony, child support, and taxes you owe. This legal protection of retirement assets allows people who lose most of what they own through bankruptcy, yet keep over a million dollars in retirement accounts untouched. It is an especially valuable feature for small business owners, in my opinion. But unfortunately, many small business owners seem to be too focused on saving pennies and dimes and don't set up a retirement plan because of costs.

Added Benefits for Education Planning

Though it may seem that retirement planning is independent of education planning, well-planned retirement savings can significantly affect your education planning. Colleges and universities require students complete

FAFSA (Free Application for Federal Student Aid) to be considered for financial aid including federally funded student loans and grants. For students with little or no income, parents' income and assets determine their chance to receive financial aid with better conditions. The number of scholarships and grants, interest rates, repayment terms, etc. can be based on the parents' finances. As for parents' assets, some are excluded in financial aid calculation. Primary home, even if it is all paid for, and retirement assets are the two most significant exclusions. No matter how much you have in your retirement accounts, they are not generally considered as assets for your children's education.

Other assets such as money in checking/savings accounts, CDs, and non-retirement accounts will directly affect the amount of financial aid your child may receive, though some amounts are exempted. For example, if you have $500,000 in your 401(k), no amount will affect potential financial aid for your child, while the same amount in a non-retirement account will. Financial assistance can be vastly different for students whose parents have similar income and assets, depending on types of accounts that hold their assets. As you know, all qualified retirement accounts have maximum limits for yearly contributions. By maximally funding for your retirement, you may increase your child's chance of receiving preferred financial aid. Unless you can pay for your child's education without any help, I strongly recommend starting to plan for your retirement and your children's education as soon as possible.

Chapter 5 | RETIREMENT PLANNING

Individual Retirement Accounts

Traditional IRA and Roth IRA

People with earned income (money made from working) can open an IRA (Individual Retirement Account) and contribute up to $5,500 or $6,500 if 50 or older ($6,000 or $7,000 in 2019). They can open either or both Traditional IRA and Roth IRA and contribute to either or both accounts, but the total contribution for both accounts has to be within the yearly limit. See the following table for differences between two IRAs.

Features	Traditional IRA	Roth IRA
Who can contribute?	Anyone (including spouse) who has earned income but younger than 70 ½	Anyone who has earned income at any age, if MAGI is within the limits
Deductibility	Yes, if qualify	No
Maximum contribution	$5,500 ($6,500 if 50 or older) or up to earned income, whichever is smaller	
Deadline	Tax filing due date, usually mid-April	
When can I withdraw?	After 59 ½ but in theory, you can withdraw any time, though taxes and penalty may apply	
Required minimum distribution (RMD)	RMD must start once the owner becomes 70 ½	Not required for the original owner

94

| Are withdrawals taxable? | Yes, plus 10% penalty for non-qualified distributions | No, if distributions are qualified. Otherwise, taxes and penalties may apply |

Traditional IRA

Pre-Tax Contribution

As for a Traditional IRA, you can deduct the contributions, but you have to pay income taxes on all withdrawals after retirement. Please understand this: If you pay taxes now (Post-tax or Roth), your principal and all the profit, no matter how large, will be tax-free, whereas if you don't pay taxes now (Pre-tax), *both* principal and gains will be taxed after retirement. When you think about it, the actual amount of taxes you pay on Roth accounts in which you pay taxes only on the contribution is less than Traditional accounts where you pay taxes on both principal *and* profits when distributed. Then why would anyone prefer a Traditional IRA or any pre-tax retirement account? That is because you can utilize the money that you otherwise would have paid in taxes as your seed money and grow in Traditional IRA. The benefits may vary depending on one's circumstances and will be further discussed in the following section, Which One is Better?

Deductibility of Traditional IRA Contributions

Not all Traditional IRA contributions are deductible, however. Your deduction depends on your tax filing status, income, and whether you have a qualified retirement plan through work, regardless of your participation. If you do not have a retirement plan through work, then

Chapter 5 | RETIREMENT PLANNING

you can contribute to the yearly IRA maximum and deduct the entire amount, regardless of the income. The following table shows deductibility of those who do have a retirement plan through work. (Source: IRS.gov -*2018 IRA Deduction Limits - Effect of Modified AGI on Deduction if You Are Covered by a Retirement Plan at Work*).

If Your Filing Status Is...	And Your Modified AGI Is...	Then You Can Take...
Single or head of household	$63,000 or less	A full deduction up to the amount of your contribution limit.
	More than $63,000 but less than $73,000	a partial deduction.
	$73,000 or more	No deduction.
Married filing jointly or qualifying widow(er)	$101,000 or less	A full deduction up to the amount of your contribution limit.
	More than $101,000 but less than $121,000	A partial deduction.
	$121,000 or more	No deduction.
Married filing separately	Less than $10,000	A partial deduction.
	$10,000 or more	No deduction.

If you file separately and did not live with your spouse at any time during the year, your IRA deduction is determined under the "single" filing status.

You can find out your Modified AGI (MAGI) once you give your tax information to your accountant for tax filing or you can search online for a MAGI calculator to estimate it. If you are offered a group retirement plan through work and your MAGI limits your deductibility on a Traditional IRA contribution, consider using a Roth IRA, if eligible.

Correcting Over-Contribution

If you accidentally over-contribute into your IRA account(s), you must either re-characterize the over-contributed amount for next year's contribution or withdraw the extra principal plus any profits from it, if any. The correction must be made by the original tax file deadline, which is typically mid-April. After that, 6% tax is imposed each year until corrected.

Early Distribution Penalty

Early distributions before age 59 ½ are subject to income taxes and a 10% penalty unless exempted. Once account owners turn 70 ½, they not only cannot contribute into their Traditional IRA, but they also must start taking required minimum distributions (RMD) and pay income taxes on the withdrawals.

Roth IRA

Post-Tax Contribution

As previously explained, contributions in a Roth IRA are post-tax, meaning you cannot deduct the contribution amount for your tax purposes; however you never pay any taxes on qualified withdrawals after that, regardless of profits.

Contribution After 70 ½

Unlike a Traditional IRA in which contributions are disallowed after age 70 ½, you can continue to fund a Roth IRA as long as you have income from work.

Taxation

Because the taxes are already paid on the contribution in a Roth IRA, you can withdraw the principal amounts any time with no restrictions. Unqualified withdrawals of the earnings are taxed with an extra 10% penalty. The 10% penalty will be waived under some circumstances such as if the account owner is permanently disabled or funds are used for the 1st home purchase (up to $10,000). For more information on exceptions to early distribution penalties, visit IRS.gov (*Retirement Topics – Exceptions to Tax on Early Distributions*).

Income Limits for Roth IRA Contribution

Like there are conditions for one's Traditional IRA deductibility, there are restrictions based on one's tax filing status and income for Roth IRA contributions. See the following table:

If your filing status is...	And your MAGI is...	Then you can contribute...
Married filing jointly or qualifying widow(er)	< $189,000	Up to the limit
	> $189,000 but < $199,000	A reduced amount
	> $199,000	Zero
Married filing separately and you lived with your spouse at any time during the year	< $10,000	A reduced amount
	> $10,000	Zero

Chapter 5 | RETIREMENT PLANNING

Single, head of household, or married filing separately and you did not live with your spouse at any time during the year	< $120,000	Up to the limit
	> $120,000 but < $135,000	A reduced amount
	> $135,000	Zero

The table is from IRS.gov for year 2018 (*Amount of Roth IRA Contributions That You Can Make For 2018*). Visit the website for more information.

Backdoor Roth IRA

If you are not allowed to deduct Traditional IRA contributions and your income is too high for Roth IRA, you can consider utilizing "backdoor Roth." It is not an account, rather a method to increase retirement savings. This method is considered and criticized by many as one of the tax "loopholes" that allow the wealthy to save more in a tax-advantaged way when the majority of the people are struggling to make ends meet. There have been rumors that the Congress will close this "loophole," but it still is available as of 2018, so I'm explaining it.

The way you can utilize this involves two steps and two accounts: First, contribute into a Traditional IRA as a "non-deductible" contribution, and second, immediately transfer it to a Roth IRA. It is best if you do not have assets in an existing Traditional IRA; otherwise, there can be tax consequences. Let's say you already have $50,000 in your Traditional IRA and make a non-deductible contribution of $5,500 in the account this year to utilize backdoor Roth. The non-deductible portion of $5,500 is about 10% of the new total $55,500 in your Traditional IRA account. Even if you open a new Traditional IRA account with another institution and contribute the non-deductible $5,500, all the assets in deductible IRA accounts (including SIMPLE & SEP IRA) are totaled for the conversion purposes. For you to convert the non-deductible contribution of $5,500 into your Roth IRA, you'll end up transferring 90% of deductible assets (which is subject to income taxes) and 10% of non-deductible assets (which is not subject to taxes). In other words, of the $5,500, about $4,950 will be taxed as ordinary income, and the rest, about $550, can be transferred to a Roth IRA without tax consequences. In this case, the conversion may not make much financial sense, which is why you need further planning to avoid this unintended consequence. You can first transfer all Traditional IRA assets into your 401(k) account before contributing money as non-deductible, for example. Depending on investment options and costs in your 401(k) account, this option may not make much financial sense, either. Consult a financial planner who doesn't benefit from your decision before making any move. The reason that an impartial adviser is essential here is that anyone who *can* make money based on your Traditional IRA asset may not be motivated to advise you to move it to your 401(k) in which he or she won't make money, even if that is for your best interest.

Mega Backdoor Roth IRA

Hoping that we now all understand why utilizing tax-advantaged retirement accounts is so important to increase and protect one's hard-earned money, I want to introduce one more way that can allow people to save extra tens of thousands of dollars into a Roth IRA. It is called the mega backdoor Roth IRA, though it is not an official name, as this method of saving is not very official or widely known.

As for the backdoor Roth IRA, anyone with earned income (and a pre-tax retirement account through work) can do it with some planning. Mega backdoor Roth IRA requires two specific conditions in their 401(k): the plan must allow after tax, non-Roth contributions *and* in-service distribution. If a plan permits in-service distribution, participants can transfer some of their entire 401(k) asset to another retirement account while working for the company. Most retirement plan management companies make money based on the amount of the plan assets, so the more money there is inside of the plan, the more they make in general. It is not likely that plan managers would actively recommend in-service distribution as an option at the time of the plan setup. However, a plan sponsor (your company) can change the plan options, so you can request it if necessary. (Don't be shy to raise your voice if it can also benefit other people in your company). If you are a small business owner, first consult with your financial planner or the third-party administrator (TPA) for your 401(k) plan to see if this can work for you. Depending on your employees' participation in the plan, your extra contributions may be limited.

The way it works is similar to the backdoor Roth IRA in which you make non-deductible and non-Roth contributions and quickly transfer the money to your Roth IRA account. Like in the backdoor Roth IRA, it works best if you can do it almost simultaneously because you have to pay taxes on the profits, if any, before the money is transferred into the Roth account. The maximum you can contribute is $55,000 ($61,000 if 50 or older) minus any company match. For example, say you, 45 years old, save $18,500 into your 401(k), and your company contributes a total of $10,000 in the match and profit sharing in a given year. Then you can save extra up to $26,500 (55,000-18,500-10,000) as a non-deductible and non-Roth contribution in your 401(k) from your paycheck and immediately transfer that amount to your Roth IRA. This mega backdoor Roth IRA "trick" is not allowed in other retirement plans such as SIMPLE IRA but may be allowed in 403(b) plans. Check your plan documents to see if your plan allows non-deducible and non-Roth contribution as well as in-service distribution. If you have an owner-only 401(k), which is for a small business without any employees who work more than 1,000 hours a year, you can set up the plan options for this purpose and take full advantage.

Which IRA Is Better?

Assuming you are eligible to contribute to both IRA accounts, you may wonder which one is better for you. The answer depends on your circumstances and future tax policy that we cannot foresee.

Tax deductions are worth more when you are in a higher income tax bracket: the higher your income tax rates and the more you save for retirement (within limits), the higher the tax savings you will get from deductions. One of the keys to whether you should save in Roth or Traditional IRA account is based on your potential tax benefits from deductions. For those in high income tax brackets, saving taxes now (Traditional IRA) is typically recommended. If your income is at peak, pre-tax (Traditional IRA) can be better, assuming the future tax rates would be the same or similar to today's. If you just started working and expect your income to grow from now, or if your income in any given year is significantly lower than usual, or if you expect your income tax rates are likely to be much higher in the near future, it would make more sense to save post-tax in a Roth account (Roth IRA or Roth 401k). If you have other deductions that can significantly lower your current tax liabilities in any given year, then your extra deduction from retirement savings may not be as high as other years. In this case, saving in a Roth account may be more beneficial. All we can do is to contribute to whichever is better today and adjust it as situations change. That is why it is important, in my opinion, for you to closely work with an accountant and a financial planner. As previously stated, you can contribute to either or both IRA accounts, as long as the total amount is within yearly limits.

Regardless of which IRA you decide to utilize, you can make the contribution by the tax filing due date, which is mid-April. For example, you can decide to make IRA contributions for this year by the time you file taxes before the middle of April next year. Even if you already filed your taxes early this year without any IRA contribution, you can still contribute to the maximum for the year and file an amendment by the tax due date in April. The tax savings from deductions, in case of Traditional IRA, may outweigh the cost for the amendment filing.

HSA (Health Savings Account)

As explained in the Health Insurance section, you can effectively pay medical expenses tax-free by utilizing an HSA (health savings account). An HSA can also be used as an excellent tool for tax savings and retirement savings, which is why I further discuss it in this chapter.

Eligibility and Contributions

Like retirement accounts, there are maximum HSA contribution limits, which are $6,900 for family and $3,450 for a single person in 2018. An extra $1,000 contribution is allowed for people 55 or older, but you no longer can contribute once you turn age 65. To be qualified to contribute to an HSA, you need to have a high deductible health plan (HDHP) with a minimum deductible of $2,700 for family ($1,350 for single) and a maximum out-of-pocket limit of $13,300 for family ($6,650 for single) in 2018. Your insurance can be through your job or be obtained individually. Co-op medical aid programs such as Medi-Share and Christian Med-Aid that are through non-profit organizations won't qualify. For detailed information on HSAs, visit IRS.gov and navigate from the menu on the left side (*Publication 969 (2017), Health Savings Accounts and Other Tax-Favored Health Plans*).

Broad Definition of Qualified Medical Expenses

HSA's definition of a qualified medical expense is much broader than what typical health insurance covers. You can use your HSA funds not only for medical expenses and copay but also for over-the-counter medicine such as painkiller and eye and dental services such as eyeglasses and dentures. You can even use your HSA funds for a weight loss program if your doctor orders you to lose weight for health reasons. If you need to improve your house so you can move around in a wheelchair, you can use your HSA funds to pay for the work, too.

Effective "Discounts"

Both my sons had a dental correction (braces) that was over $10,000 in total, and it is paid from my HSA funds. As you know, HSA contributions are tax deductible, and since the dental correction was a qualified medical expense, no income tax was paid on the distribution, either. Recall that all retirement savings are taxed either before contribution (Roth) or at distribution (all non-Roth accounts). In my HSA case, no taxes were ever paid. If my effective income tax rate was 25%, paying for my sons' dental correction from HSA funds resulted in the same as savings of $2,500 from the $10,000 total costs! That is what makes HSAs better than qualified retirement contributions when it comes to tax savings. As one instructor from a class during my study for a CFP® exam once jokingly put it, HSAs are like "IRAs with cocaine."

Investment Options

Many HSAs offer mutual fund investment options, which effectively allow you to treat HSA funds as retirement assets because the money can grow without any tax consequences. Depending on financial institution you have your HSA account, investment options and costs may differ. See the *HSA comparison chart* on HSASearch.com for monthly fees and investment options, but verify the accuracy before opening an account.

Medical Expense Reimbursement

If you forget to use your HSA debit card for medical expense, you can reimburse it to yourself from your HSA account later. The reimbursement can be easily made in a check or direct deposit into your bank account from your HSA account. But the burden of proving that amount as a qualified medical expense is on you, so be sure to keep the receipt that matches the reimbursement amount. IRS may ask you to provide the proof some years after you file your taxes.

Using your HSA debit card directly at medical institutions is, of course, most recommended. If you are buying over-the-counter medicine, which is a qualified medical expense for HSA, and food at Wal-Mart, for example, pay for the drug separately using the HSA card.

That way, the end-of-year tax document that you'll receive from the HSA company shows the distributions as qualified medical expenses, and you won't have to do anything other than reporting it as a qualified distribution when filing taxes.

Non-Qualified Distributions

Like qualified retirement assets, nothing stops you from withdrawing HSA funds anytime you want and use it for non-medical expense purposes, such as for vacation. It is in fact easy to make non-qualified distributions because you have an HSA debit card on your hand that can be mistaken for another credit card. The penalty for a non-qualified HSA distribution is higher at 20% than a non-qualified distribution from most retirement accounts, which is 10%.

No Penalty after 65 & No RMD

If you make non-qualified distributions after age 65, however, the penalty is waived. At that time, your HSA becomes like a retirement account with pre-tax contributions. But it is still better because there's no required minimum distribution (RMD) on HSA accounts, effectively allowing you to grow your money as long as you live. You don't have to use HSA funds for medical expenses if you can afford it. I hope you fully understand now why I discuss HSAs in depth in this chapter for retirement planning. I recommend my clients to mostly treat their HSA as an extra retirement account that can *also* be used for medical expenses, tax-free. The same instructor that I mentioned earlier saying how great an HSA was also said that if he had to choose between his wife and an HSA, his wife might lose. Of course, he was joking (I hope), but you get the point.

Group Retirement Plans

There are many group retirement plans with different rules and options. In this section, I'll explain several retirement plans that are most popular.

SIMPLE IRA

Plan for Small Businesses with Employees
Savings Incentive Match Plan for Employees (SIMPLE) IRAs are commonly used for businesses with up to 100 employees. It is easy and cheap (or free) to set up, compared to 401(k) plans, and annual reporting requirements are minimal. Like all other salary deferral plans, employees are in charge of contribution and investment management.

Eligibility and Basics
Employees who have worked more than two years and made at least $5,000 a year are eligible to participate in a SIMPLE IRA. That does not mean gracious business owners cannot allow their new employees to join the plan, but if they do, there must not be any discrimination. For example, a business owner cannot let her son join the plan as a new employee while telling other employees that they need to fulfill the two-year work requirement. Like 401(k) plans, employees tell their employer, in writing, to deduct a certain percentage or amount of their income and manage their investment. Employers can choose to either match up to 3% for participants or contribute 2% for all eligible employees, regardless of their participation. The maximum salary deferral is $12,500 or $15,500 for those 50 or older ($13,000 or $16,000 in 2019).

Taxes and Penalties

All qualified distributions from retirement accounts with pre-tax contributions are subject to ordinary income tax, and all non-qualified early distributions before age 59 ½ are subject to an extra 10% penalty. There's an additional penalty that exists only in SIMPLE IRA: if any non-qualified early distribution is made before two years after the opening of a SIMPLE IRA account, the penalty increases to 25%. Most qualified retirement accounts are allowed to directly transfer without any tax or penalty consequences, for example, from 401(k) to Traditional IRA or vice versa. But SIMPLE IRAs that are open less than two years can be transferred *only to* another SIMPLE IRA. If a transfer to an account other than a SIMPLE IRA is made within two years of opening the account, it is considered to be early distribution, and 25% penalty applies. With income taxes and a 25% penalty, it hardly makes financial sense for any early distributions in SIMPLE IRAs. I don't understand any logic behind this abnormal 25% penalty, but it is what it is, so we should avoid it if possible at all. There are some exceptions to the penalty such as the account owner's disability or for medical payments up to a limit. Visit IRS.gov for more information on this subject (*SIMPLE IRA Withdrawal and Transfer Rules*).

Key Points
- For small businesses with up to 100 employees
- Easy to set up with minimal report requirements: plan must be set up (Form 5305-SIMPLE must be signed) by October 1 to contribute for that year.
- Maximum contribution: $12,500 or $15,500 for those 50 or older ($13,000 or $16,000 in 2019)
- Must include all employees of two years of service who make

$5,000 or more/yr.

- Company match: Up to 3% match for contributions or 2% for all eligible employees, regardless of their participation.
- Participants are responsible for managing own investment.
- 10% penalty on non-qualified early distributions, but it increases to 25% if accounts have been open for less than two years. Only SIMPLE-to-SIMPLE direct transfer is allowed without penalty within the first two-year period.
- Participants can contribute as long as they are employed, but they must start taking required minimum distributions (RMDs) once they turn 70 ½.

For more information on SIMPLE IRA, visit IRS.gov (*SIMPLE IRA Plan*).

SEP IRA

Hybrid between Pension and Salary Deferral Plans

Simplified Employee Pension (SEP) IRAs are a hybrid between costly traditional pension plans and more modern and less expensive plans such as SIMPLE IRAs and 401(k)s. Like traditional pension plans, employers fund SEP IRAs, though it is discretionary, meaning the employers can contribute *if* they want to. Like SIMPLE IRAs and 401(k)s, employees in SEP IRA plans are responsible for investment management. In other words, employers put money in employees' SEP accounts, if they want to, but they are *not* responsible for managing investments. Like SIMPLE IRAs, SEPs are easy to set up and have minimal reporting requirements.

The shifting of asset management by employees from employers is an important distinction between traditional pension plans and today's more common salary deferral retirement plans because employers could eliminate many burdens that come with pension plans. In pension plans, as explained previously, employers are responsible for asset accumulation, management, and distribution of benefits to retirees. All funds are kept and managed in one account, and an actuary is consulted to determine how much the sponsors (employers) have to contribute each year to deliver promised benefits to retirees. That means companies have to contribute more if the securities markets drop or if more benefits are paid out than expected. Employers with a SEP IRA plan can just put money into the eligible employees' accounts, if they want to, leaving all the rest burdens to the employees.

Because SEP IRAs are funded by employers, they are preferred by small companies that employ mostly families and close members.

Eligibilities and Basics

Any employee who is at least 21 years old and has worked three years in the past five years making $600/yr. or more, and is expected to make that amount or more this year must be included in SEP IRAs. Nothing stops employers from being more generous and including all employees regardless of age or duration of employment, as long as the same rule applies to all employees. The maximum discretionary contribution is 25% of gross income up to $55,000 ($56,000 in 2019). There is no catch-up for 50 or older because it is not a salary deferral plan. The contributions for owners are calculated differently, but for owners of corporations (S or C), the maximum is the same as other employees at 25% of their w-2 gross income. An owner or not, the maximum contribution is $55,000 ($56,000 in 2019). Traditional IRAs can be added to a SEP IRA plan so participants can contribute from their wage up to $5,500 or $6,500 for those 50 or older ($6,000 or $7,000 in 2019).

Key Points
- Small business pension plan that can be set up by the tax-filing deadline (including extension).
- Employers contribute up to 25% of employee's gross income up to a total of $55,000 ($56,000 in 2019).
- Account owners are responsible for asset management.
- Must include employees who are 21 years old, worked at least three years of the past five years, and earn $600/yr. or more.
- Contributions can be made for participants after age 70 ½, but required minimum distributions (RMDs) must be taken after account owners turn 70 ½.
- All qualified distributions are subject to income tax, but for non-qualified distributions before 59 ½, an extra 10% penalty applies.

For more information on SEP, visit IRS.gov (*Simplified Employee Pension Plan*).

401(k) Plans

Salary Deferral Plan with Many Options

As previously mentioned, 401(k) plans became popular in an effort for employers to solve issues with increasing financial liabilities of traditional pension plans. Although 401(k) plans are much cheaper than pension plans to provide in general, they are more complex and costly, compared to other small business plans such as SIMPLE IRA. So they are mostly used by mid-to-large businesses these days, as for companies with more than 100 employees, a 401(k) is about the only retirement plan option that is cost effective. Small business owners with a few employees may prefer a 401(k) plan in spite of complexity and costs for many options available in 401(k)s but not in IRAs (SIMPLE or SEP). I'll further discuss this later. The name, 401(k), is from an IRS tax code.

Eligibility

All employees who are 21 or older and have worked for one year (or 1,000 hours) must be allowed to participate in a 401(k) plan. These are minimum requirements, meaning a plan can be generous and include all new employees, regardless of age or time of service. Once employees become eligible, they stay eligible even if their hours are reduced to less than 1,000 in any given year.

Contribution

Participants can save up to $18,500 **or** $24,500 for those 50 or older ($19,000 or $25,000 in 2019) from their payroll, and employers can match up to a certain percentage and have a profit sharing option inside of the plan. Employer match can vary, but I commonly see somewhere between 3-6%. The maximum employer match, including profit sharing, can be up to 25% of employees' salaries, but a total contribution from employees and their employer cannot be more $55,000 or $61,000 for those 50 or older ($56,000 or $62,000 in 2019).

 The same 1% match will give more dollars for higher earners than low-wage workers in the same plan, of course. The government put a limit on the compensation for that purpose, which is $275,000 ($280,000 in 2019). Business owners can pay themselves much higher compensation than that, of course, but for the employer's contribution calculation purposes, this is the maximum that can be used. This limit applies to other salary deferral plans such as 403(b) and SIMPLE IRA, as well as profit sharing plans and SEP IRA. Depending on ownership and some other conditions, the compensation may be further limited. Visit IRS.gov for more information on this subject (*COLA Increases for Dollar Limitations on Benefits and Contributions*).

Distribution

All pre-tax retirement contributions and profits are taxable as ordinary income for the year of distribution. If non-qualified distributions are made from your 401(k) account before 59 ½, an extra penalty of 10% is applied. There are exceptions to this 10% penalty, and for information on this topic, visit IRS.gov (*Retirement Topics - Exceptions to Tax on Early Distributions*)

After Age 70 ½

You can continue to save into your 401(k) account as long as you're eligible, regardless of age. You can also delay required minimum distributions (RMD), which is a benefit that is not available in IRA-based retirement plans. Owners with more than 5% ownership cannot delay RMD after 70 ½, although they can continue saving, as long as they are working.

Loan Feature

One of many features that 401(k) plan sponsors (employers) can have in their plan is a loan option. It is also available for other plans such as, but not limited to, 403(b) and 457(b) but not for small plans such as SIMPLE and SEP IRAs. The maximum loan amount can be either $50,000 or 50% of the vested balance, whichever is smaller. A loan must be paid off within five years or immediately upon termination of service. Otherwise, the unpaid loan amount can be treated as a distribution, which then would cause unexpected tax liability and possibly an extra 10% penalty. For more information on this topic, visit IRS.gov (*Retirement Topics – Plan Loans*).

While the loan option to utilize your retirement funds may sound good, I generally discourage business owners from implementing one, which is within their power. The reason for it is because I have yet to see anyone who borrowed from his or her retirement account and not regret it later. Of course, that doesn't mean that there aren't some people who successfully utilized a 401(k) loan for their advantage in the long run. It certainly can work better than having to take an early distribution. However, having a loan option available seems to work as irresistible poisonous candy for many people. Treat retirement assets as they are intended for, and don't borrow from your own future. That is why having emergency funds is so important and should be your top financial goal.

Vesting Schedule

Another feature that 401(k) plans can have is a vesting schedule. It is a condition that employers impose on their contribution usually in years of service before their contribution is vested, meaning employees can take it when they leave the company. Employees' own contributions are, of course, 100% vested at all times. All employer contributions in SIMPLE and SEP IRAs are also immediately vested 100%. Two typical vesting schedule types are a three-year cliff and six-year graded vesting. If your plan has a three-year cliff, employer's contributions are fully vested after three years of service and nothing before then. If you have a six-year graded vesting schedule, you will get 20% vested after one year of service, 40% after two years, 60% after three years… and finally, 100% vested after six years of working for the company. If you leave the company before fully vested, you lose the unvested amount and the profits from it, which can be substantial. All employer contributions must be fully vested in case of plan (not employment) termination or upon participants' normal retirement age, which the plan defines.

Traditional 401(k) vs. Safe Harbor 401(k)

When you work for a company that offers a 401(k) plan, it is likely either a Traditional or Safe Harbor 401(k) plan. Traditional 401(k) plans allow more control in employer contributions but can limit owners' (and possibly managers') own contributions, while Safe Harbor 401(k) plans offer limited control on employer contributions but do not limit owners' (and possibly managers') contributions.

Traditional 401(k)

Companies with a traditional 401(k) plan have great control over their contributions. For example, they can have a lower match at 1%, and even that is discretionary. In other words, they don't have to contribute anything if they don't want to, and for whatever they do contribute for their employees, they can place a vesting schedule on it. The tradeoff of the control/flexibility is that all Traditional 401(k) plans must pass additional non-discrimination tests. If a company fails the test(s), either it has to give an extra contribution for the participants, or owners (and possibly managers) have to withdraw their contributions to correct it. This rule is in place by the government to stop business owners from taking advantage of bells and whistles that come with 401(k) mainly for themselves.

Safe Harbor 401(k)

Safe Harbor 401(k) plans, on the other hand, cannot place a vesting schedule on Safe Harbor match, but they can on other employer contributions such as profit sharing and stock options. A Safe Harbor 401(k) match has to be either 3% for *all* eligible employees, regardless of their participation, or a match up to 4% for participating employees. If companies have either or both a profit sharing plan and stock options, they *can* place a vesting schedule of their choice. For example, let's say that your employer has contributed $2,000 for a Safe Harbor match and $1,500 for Profit Sharing for you for a total of $3,500. If you decide to leave the company tomorrow, you can take the $2,000 Safe Harbor match and the profits from it without any restriction. You may or may not be able to take the $1,500 Profit Sharing contribution plus earnings from it, depending on the plan's set up. Needless to say, you should check your vesting status before changing a job.

Why Small Business Should Consider 401(k)

As mentioned earlier, 401(k) plans are complex, and costs are higher than SEP and SIMPLE IRAs, but I recommend small business owners with employees to consider a Safe Harbor 410(k) if they could save more than the SIMPLE IRA limit. The employee contribution limit in a 401(k) is higher at $18,500 or $24,500 if 50 or older ($19,000 or $25,000 in 2019), compared to a SIMPLE IRA at $12,500 or $15,500 if 50 or older ($13,000 or $15,000 in 2019). In addition, 401(k) plans can have an optional profit sharing plan inside of it with up to a 25% total employer contribution. SIMPLE and SEP IRAs cannot have an attached profit sharing plan. Depending on the income and discretionary employer contribution in a 401(k) plan, married couples who run a small business together can save over $100,000 in total, all of which is tax deductible and is protected from general creditors. This tax deduction and asset protection features are great benefits that are allowed in qualified retirement plans but not available in non-retirement accounts. The amount protected from general creditors is unlimited in qualified employer-sponsored retirement plans, whereas it may be limited for individual retirement accounts such as a Traditional IRA and a Roth IRA. No such protection is available in assets in personal bank accounts and regular brokerage accounts. Maximizing savings and sheltering those assets in a retirement account is needlessly a great strategy to one's financial stability. It is especially true, in my opinion, for small business owners who potentially face greater financial risks with higher failure rates than large corporations.

If you are unable to save more than SIMPLE IRA contribution limits, however, it would make more financial sense to do SIMPLE. You can later start a 401(k) and transfer the SIMPLE IRA assets when you can save more.

Key Points

- Eligibility: 21 years of age and one year of service (1,000 hours).
- Maximum Employee Salary Deferral: $18,500 or $24,500 if 50 or older ($19,000 or $25,000 in 2019).
- Employer Contribution: up to 25% or $55,000 ($61,000 if 50 or older), including employee contribution ($56,000 or $62,000 in 2019).
- All qualified distributions are taxed as ordinary income.
- An extra 10% penalty is applied for non-qualified distribution before 59 ½ but is waived for those who take distributions after termination of service after age 55. 401(k) assets that are transferred into a Traditional IRA after employment termination lose the penalty exemption.

- Employees can continue to save after 70 ½ *and* delay RMD. Owners with 5% or more ownership cannot delay RMD but can continue saving.

403(b) Plans

403(b) plans are very similar to 401(k) plans, with the most significant difference being that they are for nonprofit organizations such as schools, hospitals, and charities. The name comes from the IRS tax code. Many nonprofit organizations offer 403(b) on top of an existing pension plan. Based on fiscal problems that so many pension plans face today, it's inevitable that more nonprofit organizations will offer a salary deferral plan like 403(b) while reducing pension benefits.

Traditionally, 403(b)s were offered through annuities with limited investment options, but many are becoming similar to 401(k)s with various mutual fund investment options. The catch-up (the extra amount that older employees age 50 or older can save) is the same as 401(k)s at $6,000 (2018 & 2019). Additionally, 403(b) plans can allow an extra catch-up for their participants: $3,000 per year up to a total of $15,000 for those who have worked more than 15 years and have saved less than $5,000/yr. It is called the 15-year rule and can help employees close to retirement accelerate savings. For employees who are eligible for both catch-ups, the maximum they could contribute would be $27,500 ($18,500+$6,000+$3,000) in 2018 ($28,000 in 2019). The employer can contribute up to 25% of the employees' income, but the total from employee and employer contributions cannot be more than $55,000 or $61,000 if 50 or older ($56,000 or $62,000 in 2019). Since 403(b) plans are for not-for-profit organizations, they cannot have a profit sharing plan.

Distribution rules on 403(b) plans are very similar to 401(k) plans. For more information on 403(b) plans, visit IRS.gov (*Tax-Sheltered 403(b) Plan Basics*)

Profit Sharing Plans

For-profit companies can have a profit sharing plan either attached to a 401(k) plan or as a separate plan. As the name indicates, contributions are made by employers to share profits with employees. They can be either or both cash and company stocks with restrictions. If it is cash, the plan may allow employees to choose if they want to receive the benefit as cash or deposit it to be invested for retirement. If cash is received, taxes must be paid. If it is deposited into employees' accounts and invested for retirement, then income taxes on principal and profits from the plan are deferred until withdrawals. I strongly recommend people have it invested for retirement instead of taking it in cash unless they already maximize the annual employee contribution from the payroll. This is a great way to save income taxes and bump up retirement savings.

Pension Plans

Pension benefits can vary, depending on how they are set up. With pension plans, there isn't much that employees need to do, as contributions, investment management, and distribution of benefits are responsibilities of the employers. Even if an organization is not profitable in any given year, pension contributions must be made. You should, of course, know what the plan benefits are, and the best way to find that out is to read the plan documents or ask the person in charge of the plan.

No matter how good your current pension benefits are, however, keep in mind that they may not last until the end of your lifetime. I recommend you prepare as if your benefits would be reduced to avoid a financial pitfall at a later age.

Other Plans

So far, I've talked about several qualified retirement plans that provide excellent tax benefits for both employers and employees. You may then wonder if there are non-qualified retirement plans. Yes, there are, and non-qualified plans can be set up for an organization independently from a qualified plan, whereas two qualified retirement plans generally cannot be offered for the same employees at the same time. One of the problems with qualified retirement plans is that the maximum contribution by both employees and their employer is limited to $55,000 or $61,000 for those 50 or older in popular salary deferral plans such as 401(k) and 403(b) ($56,000 or $62,000 in 2019). SEP IRA is limited to $55,000 ($56,000 in 2019) for all ages because it is a pension plan paid by the employer and employees cannot make $6,000 catch-up contribution. And SIMPLE IRAs have even lower total contribution limits at $12,500 or $15,500 for those 50 or older ($13,000 or $16,000 in 2019). While these amounts are a dream number for retirement savings for so many people, it may not be enough for those with high income to fully fund their retirement needs.

Non-qualified retirement plans don't have limits on contribution and require fewer rules to follow. They can selectively choose who can participate and impose strict vesting rules, unlike qualified retirements plans that have much stricter rules against eligibility discrimination and limited vesting schedules. The assets may even be vulnerable to creditors of the company, unlike qualified retirement plan assets that are protected. Usually, contributions on non-qualified retirement plans are not tax-deductible, but they can grow tax-deferred if some requirements are met. Organizations can contribute cash, stocks, insurance policies, etc., for the benefit of selected employees, usually for executive officers or organization leaders. I won't go into details in explaining non-qualified plans, as this book is intended for most people who are not likely to be offered such plan. One that is worth mentioning, in my view, is a 457(b).

A 457(b) plan is somewhere between qualified and non-qualified retirement plans. It is usually offered to government and nonprofit organization employees who are in a managerial position. The maximum employee contribution limit on 457(b) is the same as in 401(k) and 403(b) plans, and it *is* tax deductible. Because 457(b) is independent from a qualified plan, an eligible organization *can* provide a 457(b) plan along with a qualified plan such as 403(b) or 401(k), and participants can independently contribute to each plan's maximum limit. If both 401(k) and 403(b) were offered at the same time, however, the participants' total contribution is limited to $18,500 or $24,500 for those 50 or older ($19,000 or $25,000). A 457(b) plan can also provide an excellent special catch-up contribution up to the annual employee contribution limit for employees who are within three years of retirement. Assume that you, 62 and expected to retire in three years, are eligible to participate in 457(b) and 403(b) plans. Also further assume that you are eligible to contribute an extra $3,000 based on your 403(b) plan's 15-year-rule, and your 457(b) plan allows a double contribution for participants who are within three years from retirement. Then you can defer your salary close to $60,000 in total ($18,500

+$3,000 for 403(b) plus $18,500x2 for 457(b)). Because 457(b) plans are non-qualified, many rules in qualified retirement plans don't apply when it comes to contribution limits and distributions. Because contributions are tax-deductible, all distributions are taxed as ordinary income, but there are no early distribution penalties or RMD in 457(b). This is quite a benefit for government and nonprofit organization employees, don't you think? If you are lucky enough to be offered these, take full advantage if you can. And if you are working at a nonprofit organization that is eligible for a 457(b) plan but do not yet have one, lobby your bosses, as this can greatly benefit them as well.

What Participants (Employees) Need to Know

Take the "Free Money"

If your company offers a match, make sure you contribute whatever is required to take the maximum advantage of the "free money." Conditions on a match may sound somewhat confusing. An example may be like 100% up to 3% and 50% up to 6% over 3% of participants' contributions. What it says is that the company will match dollar-for-dollar up to 3% of your first contribution and 50% of your next 4-6% contribution, yielding the maximum company match up to 4.5%. For you to take that maximum 4.5% match, you must minimally contribute 6% of your income per pay period. If you are not sure, ask the person who's in charge of your plan how much you need to save to get the maximum match. Even if 6% seems too much for you to start, I strongly recommend you try it first. See how much less money you take home and how your savings accumulate for a few years. The difference of your net pay may be surprisingly smaller than you think, and the increasing balance from your savings plus the company match, a total of 10.5% in this scenario, along with extra investment profits, hopefully, will motivate you to continue the savings. For most people, this is the best and possibly the only way to achieve financial stability. Not taking maximum advantage of the match is like saying *NO* to a 4.5% raise. Please don't do that.

If Your Plan Has High Fees

When you are offered a company retirement plan, you don't have much control over the fees and options, and if you are working for a relatively small company, there is a good chance that your plan has investment options with higher fees. That is not to say all large company plans have lower fees than average. I've seen small and large 401(k) plans with abnormal fees. For employees with high 401(k) fees, I generally recommend them to contribute the minimum that is required to take the company match, if any, and save the rest in an IRA, instead. For them, it worked well because all they could save was the 401(k) match requirement and the maximum IRA contribution, anyway. For those who *can* save more, this situation can be a more serious problem because their 401(k) may be the only option that allows them to get more tax benefits for retirement savings. If you find yourself in this situation, be more active in reducing the fees. Your company (the sponsor) has the fiduciary duty to check if fees in the plans are "reasonable." The laws don't specify a range for "reasonable fees," but an article on USAToday.com says that an average 401(k) plan fees are about 1% (*Ask a Fool: How much should my 401(k) cost in fees?*).

Most 401(k) plans have fees that are embedded in mutual funds, on top of a fixed annual account maintenance fee. Identifying investment fees can be confusing because they are not on the statement, and different funds have different fees embedded in the products. So depending on your investment selections, what you pay can be significantly different from what your co-workers in the same plan pay. You can find mutual fund fees by searching each fund on the Internet. Type the name of the funds that are in your plan, and don't forget the funds' class such as A, B, C, etc. If it is difficult for you to determine if your plan fees are "reasonable," consult a financial planner who has experience in retirement plans.

Once you determine that your fees are abnormal (high), don't hesitate to bring it to the person who's in charge. Then she/he must carry out the sponsor's fiduciary duty to keep reasonable expenses either by renegotiating with the current investment company or moving the plan to somewhere else. You may feel reluctant in imposing such a burden on that person, but remember that this will benefit everyone in the plan. Understanding how a seemingly small percentage of fees can significantly affect your asset accumulation is very important, so I'll discuss it more throughout the book.

What Sponsors (Owners) Need to Know

You may be surprised to hear that many financial advisors in the financial industry are salespeople who are under pressure to meet sales quotas. Many of them are not necessarily obligated to work in your best interest, while you, as a qualified retirement plan sponsor, are obligated to provide reasonable fees and carry out your duties prudently. Take your legal responsibilities seriously. If you don't, you, a qualified retirement plan sponsor, can be sued by your employees for violating your fiduciary duties. See an article that talks about it on CNBC.com (*Lousy 401(k) Plans May Spark More Lawsuits*). Also, visit DOL.gov to understand what your fiduciary duties are as a qualified retirement plan sponsor (*Meeting Your Fiduciary Responsibilities*).

Analyze your plan fees periodically and compare with those of other providers. As stated earlier, small businesses generally pay higher 401(k) fees, and there is a growing market for small business owners who are looking for better options. Employee Fiduciary is one of the service providers that are being recognized and I've used them for my clients after learning about the company from CBSnews.com (*Best Small Company 401(k) Provider*)*. I like their low and transparent fee structure, along with a variety of investment options. Their website even lets you compare your provider's fees to others (*Compare Your 401(k) Provider's Fees*). Finally, make sure you notify employees who become eligible to participate promptly and keep good records. Not prudently practicing the rules that a qualified retirement plan sponsor is supposed to follow can disqualify your plan. (*Disclaimer: I use Employee Fiduciary to set up a 401(k) plan for my clients, and I'm registered on their advisor search engine. I do not receive any type of compensation from Employee Fiduciary, as all my service fees are paid directly by my clients.)

What to Do with 401(k) When Changing Jobs

When you consider leaving your current job with a 401(k) plan, first check if all the employer match is fully vested, meaning you can take it with you. If the employer contributions are not fully vested, know the amount that you'd forfeit by leaving the company. Depending on the amount and what you can get from a new job, staying a little longer until fully vested may make financial sense.

If fully vested, you have several options with your existing 401(k) account: you can leave it where it is, move it to your new company plan, or transfer it to a Traditional IRA account. The optimal decision may depend on some variables. If you like your (to be) old 401(k) plan and investment options offered, you can leave it. If your total balance is less than $5,000, however, the plan sponsor may force you out by issuing you a check. If you like your new plan or see no difference between the two, you can transfer the old account into the new one for easy management.

If you frequently change jobs, you may want to park all your assets in an IRA for convenience. Generally speaking, you can get better investment options with lower fees in an IRA than most 401(k) plans. One thing you need to consider before transferring your 401(k) to an IRA is that the asset protection from creditors on 401(k) assets are better than on IRAs. Your transferred 401(k) assets in an IRA usually keep the unlimited bankruptcy protection from most creditors, but they may be vulnerable to creditors in non-bankruptcy situations, depending on where you live. In general, this is a problem that people with high retirement assets (over $1 million) can face. If you are one of the lucky ones with a high balance in your 401(k) account and especially if you're vulnerable to potential lawsuits from creditors, you may want to consider keeping it in a 401(k) even if it costs you more than if transferred to an IRA. Also, if you are in a high-income bracket and want to utilize a "backdoor Roth IRA" (explained earlier in the Individual Accounts section), leaving the money in a 401(k) account will provide the maximum efficiency.

If and when you move your retirement assets from one account to another, make sure you do it directly company-to-company. If you do an indirect transfer or rollover, in which you get a check from one institution, deposit it into your personal account, and later send a check of the same amount to the new institution, there's room for trouble. In this case, you must put the money into the other retirement account within 60 days. If you miss the 60-day window or deposit less amount than the original check, then it becomes a distribution and you must pay taxes. If you're younger than 59 ½, you may have to pay an extra 10% penalty. Direct transfer from company-to-company eliminates such a potential headache and makes your life much easier.

If you want to move your 401(k) assets to an IRA account but are not sure where to go, consult a financial planner who is *not* in a position to affect your decision for his/her commission.

Starting a Retirement Plan

If you are a business owner with no retirement plan, please start one as soon as fiscally possible. I've seen many small business owners who are just too focused on the costs and ignore the benefits that they'll get from a qualified retirement plan. If you are one of them, please understand that the potential tax savings, the power of compounding, and your retirement asset protection from most creditors could easily outweigh the costs.

Of course, there's an IRA, but the maximum contribution limit in IRAs is not enough for most people's necessary retirement savings. You can save and invest in non-retirement accounts, but they are not as tax-efficient or well protected from general creditors as retirement accounts. In my opinion, providing a retirement plan is also the right thing to do for your employees who otherwise are highly limited in their retirement savings options. Most of all, remember that you, the owner, can get the greatest benefits from your company retirement plan.

Owners Only Business

So which plan should you choose? If you do not have any employee who works for more than 1,000 hours (about 20 hours per week), you can start an Individual 401(k), which is also called Self-employed 401(k), Owner-only K, Solo K, etc. Self-employed professionals without employees such as realtors, painters, and IT contractors would be good candidates for this plan. If you own two companies, one without employees and one with full time employees, then you must treat both companies as one in choosing a retirement plan. The contribution limits and other features are very similar to regular 401(k) with employees. One thing you should know is that since it is an owner-only retirement plan, your asset protection rules follow your state laws. In other words, Solo 401(k) assets would be treated like individual IRAs with a limited amount to be protected, unlike other retirement plans that are protected without a limit. Still, IRAs are protected over $1 millions in most states, so focus on maximizing the savings in the beginning.

Family Business with High Revenue

If you have a small company mainly with partners and family members that you like to share the profits with, you may want to consider SEP IRA with a Traditional IRA attached. In it, the company pays up to 25% of employees' wage to the maximum of $55,000 ($56,000 in 2019), and employees can defer their salary up to a Traditional IRA limit which is $5,500 or $6,500 for people 50 or older ($6,000 or $7,000 in 2019). A SEP IRA can be most effective for owners with high income. If your business income is not high, therefore SEP IRA contribution rate is low, you may benefit more from a salary deferral plan like Owner-only K or SIMPLE IRA.

Small Business with Employees

If you have employees and want to minimize plan costs and reporting, a SIMPLE IRA is a good choice. You can later change it to a 401(k) plan, but watch out for the 2-year rule: if you move your plan into another plan within two years of starting it, there's a 25% penalty. If you can save more than SIMPLE IRA contribution limits, a Safe Harbor 401(k) may work best for you. Small nonprofit organizations such as churches and temples can start a SEP or SIMPLE IRA plan for their paid employees, too.

Don't Forget to Claim $500 Credit

Regardless of what you decide to start with, don't forget to claim $500 tax credit (IRS Form 8881) from the first $1,000 fees that you directly pay to a 401(k) plan provider or financial planner who helps you set it up (2018). You can claim this tax credit on plan costs for the first three years of plan establishment, which is yet another way of the government incentivizing small companies (100 or less employees) to start a retirement plan.

Social Security

Funded by Workers via Payroll Taxes

The OASDI (Old Age, Survivors, and Disability Insurance), commonly known as Social Security (SS), is the largest social program that covers 96% of Americans. Everyone who has earned income (money earned from working) pays payroll taxes also known as FICA (Federal Insurance Contributions Act). The payroll taxes are currently 7.65%, of which 6.2% is for SS, and 1.45% is for Medicare. Other income such as dividends, rental income, and capital gains are not categorized as earned income, therefore not subject to payroll taxes. For this reason, people without earned income cannot receive credits for Social Security and Medicare benefits, either.

Cap for SS Tax

There's a cap for the amount of earned income, which is currently $128,400 for the Social Security tax purposes ($132,900 in 2019)). What it means is that the maximum SS tax anyone can pay is $7,961 ($8,240 in 2019). If you make less, you pay 6.2% of the total earned income, and if you make more, you pay the limited maximum, even if you make over $1 million. Employers pay the same amount, so if you are self-employed, you pay double that amount, although 50% of that is tax-deductible.

10 Years and 40 Credits

For you and your surviving family to be qualified for SS benefits, you need to work at least 10 years and pay into the SS funds. To be more specific, you need 40 credits, which will take at least 10 years to earn.

Workers can earn up to four credits per year by making (and paying SS taxes on) $5,280 ($5,440 in 2019) or more. Less (1-3) credits can be earned if you work part-time at $1,320 per credit. Required credits for SS disability benefits (SSDI) depend on the age of disability, being less for younger people and increasing to minimum 20 credits for age 31 or older. Check SSA.gov for more information on SS credits (*How You Earn Credits*).

Retirement Age

The normal retirement age that one could receive Social Security retirement benefits without a penalty was 65 at the beginning of the program but has gradually increased to 67. For those who were born before 1954, it is 66, and from there, it increases by two months each year, and for those who were born in or after 1960, it is 67. Visit SSA.gov for more information *(Normal Retirement Age)*. Currently, the earliest age workers can apply for SS retirement benefits is 62, but the benefits will be reduced.

Calculation of Benefits

Social Security retirement benefit amounts are calculated based on the highest annual income from the last 35 out of the 40 years that you pay into the system. If you work (pay into the system) for less than 35 years before applying for benefits, say 25 years, then the 10 years would be marked as zero for benefit calculations. That would, of course, lower your benefits compared to if you worked longer. Knowing your estimated benefits is essential in retirement planning. If you already have earned 40 credits, you can check your estimated benefits on the website (SSA.gov) by creating an account. You will need your Social Security number, current and previous addresses, and other personal information such as your loan company and amounts to verify yourself. *Social Security Quick Calculator* can be used if you want to quickly estimate benefits without going through a series of verification process. Understand that the Quick Calculator will not give you a good estimate of your benefits because it does not access your earnings record.

Let's take a look at an example of estimated benefits based on different income.

Income/yr.	$30,000	$50,000	$100,000	$200,000
Benefits/mo.	$1,176	$1,615	$2,464	$2,961

The data is for wage earners born in January of 1960 and the estimated benefits received at normal retirement age of 67. The benefit amounts may differ, depending on when the data is pulled because benefits increase with inflation. According to the table, a worker who makes $30,000 per year would get about $1,176 at normal retirement age, and a person who makes $50,000 per year would get $1,615, and so on. The benefit amounts increase over time due to inflation, but the value (purchasing power) should be the same as today.

Notice that the benefit amounts between different income have a narrow range: the person with $50,000 pay gets about 2/3 of what the worker who makes $100,000 receives in SS benefits, and the person with $30,000 earning receives almost half of the one with $100,000 salary receives. That is because Social Security is a social program initially designed to stop retirees from falling into a poverty level. It also means that the Social Security benefits that people with higher income receive are relatively smaller compared to what they pay into the system versus those with lower income pay and receive, which is why there is a cap in place at $128,400 as of 2018 ($132,900 in 2019).

Family Benefits

On top of monthly income for retired primary workers, Social Security provides benefits to the workers' family, too. In the case of a primary worker's premature death, his or her surviving minor children and their caregiver can receive benefits. A spouse who never worked can receive 50% of the spouse's benefits while both are alive, and once the primary worker dies, the surviving spouse can take over the deceased spouse's SS benefits. Even a divorced spouse can claim benefits based on the ex-spouse's work history if the marriage lasted over 10 years, and the claiming ex-spouse is unmarried at the time of the application.

Payments Adjusted to Inflation

Another great feature of SS benefits is that the payments are adjusted to inflation. It is a powerful feature that many pension plans and annuities don't offer. If your benefits don't get adjusted to inflation, what you are promised today could be worth much less in the future. Let's say that $3,500/mo. may be enough to cover most of your essential living expenses now at age 40. But would it still be true when you are retired at 67? How about when you're 80 or 90? How much do you think $3,500 in 40 years can buy? Assuming annual average inflation at 2%, you will need over $7,700 in 40 years to be able to buy what you can buy with $3,500 today. Always consider how inflation can affect when you buy financial products that promise fixed income with no inflation adjustment. The benefits that they promise may sound enough today, but the actual value in the future can be significantly less over time without an inflation adjustment rider.

When to Start Taking Benefits

Bonus for Waiting

If you delay taking your benefits after normal retirement age, you can get an increased amount by 8% annually until age 70. For example, say your normal retirement age is 67, and your benefits are $2,000/mo. If you can wait for three years until 70 before applying for benefits, then you can get 24% more, which is $2,480/mo.

Penalty for Early Withdrawals

If you take your retirement benefits early (62 is the earliest, unless you're disabled or a widow(er)), however, the benefits will be permanently reduced up to 30%. Whether you should wait until 70 to increase the benefits or take lower benefits at 62 or anything in between should be decided carefully. Many things like your current job and financial situation, expected lifespan, savings, and your health condition should be considered.

Finding the Breakpoint

Let's see an example of how you can find the optimal age for SS benefits. Say your retirement benefit at full retirement age of 67 is $2,000 a month. If you retire at 62 and start taking benefits, you'll get 30% less, which is $1,400 a month, but you'll receive $84,000 extra during the five-year period before your normal retirement age ($1,400 x 12 months x 5 years). You then can divide that number by $600 lost benefits per month to get 140 months or 11.67 years. What it means is that your waiting until 67, instead of taking early benefits with a 30% penalty would be paid off if you live longer than 78.67 (67+11.67=78.67) years of age. The younger you die from 78.67 years of age, the more dollars you'd end up getting in SS benefits, but the longer you live from that point, the more you'll be rewarded for the wait. You can use the same calculation to find the sweet age of delaying or taking SS benefits early for different ages, but please consider your spouse's potential benefits as well if you're married. If you and your spouse have a big age gap, it usually makes financial sense for the older spouse to delay taking benefits, assuming the older spouse's SS benefits are higher than the younger spouse's. Even if you are single, it would make financial sense to apply for SS benefits as late as you can afford if you are healthy and from a family known with longevity. For more information on benefit calculations, visit SSA.gov (*Benefits Planner: Your Future Benefits*) or consult a financial planner who's experienced on this subject. You can visit your local SS office, too.

Taking Early Benefits while Working

Be cautious if you consider taking SS benefits before your normal retirement age while working: your SS benefits could be significantly reduced if you make over $17,040 ($17,640 in 2019). For example, let's say your normal retirement age is 67 and you start taking SS benefits this year at 63 while working. If your income is $30,000, it is $12,960 more than the SS income threshold $17,040. If the total of your SS benefits for this year is $20,000, it would be reduced by $6,480 (50% of $12,960) to $13,520. In the year you turn 67, the threshold increases to $43,360 ($46,920 in 2019) and the reduction rate decreases to 1/3 from 1/2. After your normal retirement age, you can earn as much as you want and your SS benefits won't be penalized.

Issues with Social Security

This SS program is a pay-as-you-go system, meaning what you pay in SS tax today pays for benefits for current retirees, and your benefits in the future will be paid by other workers. Like other pension plans, monies in the SS program are comingled and managed in a trust without separate individual accounts. If more taxes are collected than benefits are paid in any given year, the surplus is reserved, while reserved funds are used to fill the gap if there is a shortage. Social Security Administration will have to pay out more in retirement benefits as people live longer, and it is inevitable that reserved funds will dry out sooner or later. SSA publishes a report regarding its trust funds, and according to its 2018 report, the funds are expected to be depleted by 2034. At that point, benefits would be reduced to about 3/4, unless Congress acts to fix it.

What does that mean? That means people who (expect to) get a monthly SS check of $2,000 will be getting about $1,500 instead from sometime around 2034, assuming inaction from Congress. I cannot imagine the adverse ramification of such reductions not only for those who heavily depend on their SS benefits for survival but also for the stability of the society in which we all live.

Solutions?

Since this problem with SS is mainly due to our longevity, the solution is not simple. We can try to increase the normal retirement age, but I don't know how effective this will be because about 90% of the people who start taking SS benefits before their normal retirement age do so regardless of the hefty penalty to survive. Some people say that we should eliminate the income cap that is placed for SS tax, effectively raising taxes on everyone who makes over $128,400 ($132,900 in 2019). I honestly don't know if such a tax increase proposition can pass Congress whose majority members are millionaires. Some people argue that we should privatize Social Security and run it like a business. Well, run it like which business? A business whose focus is to maximize profits for its owners and lavishly compensates the top managers for profits, while no one takes responsibility for a loss? SSA is one of the most efficiently run government agencies with less than 1% administrative expenses, so I seriously doubt any business can beat that. Some say that we should get rid of the automatic benefit increase based on the inflation rate, which will effectively reduce benefits. As you can see, there's no one easy solution.

Surviving

Now what? People who are aware of this national retirement crisis often say that they'll work until death. They say it in desperation because they don't know how they can live after retirement. I think anyone who *can* work until death is lucky because most retirees who want to and need to work cannot find a job or are physically incapable. I hope you now understand that saving for retirement is not an option, as not eating is not an option for survival. Savings cannot wait until you get a promotion or your children finish college. Even if you are a determined saver and know you *will* start saving sometime in the future, we never know what life may throw at us tomorrow. I mean there's no "better time" to save, and we must start today, no matter how difficult you may think it is.

Retirement Planning

How Much Do I Need to Save?

Knowing how much you need to support the retirement lifestyle you desire is the first step of retirement planning. Assuming that most people want to keep their current lifestyle after retirement, it is often said that about 80% of pre-retirement income is needed. Many financial planners, including myself, advise people to assume they'd need 100% of their previous income. That is because, even if you have zero debt at retirement, it is highly likely that new medical expenses would occur as you get older. Things would change if we had an affordable national health care system with a minimal financial burden on the people, but I don't see it happening in the near future. Until then, I recommend you prepare as much as you can.

Using an 80% income needs assumption and life expectancy of 90 years, Fidelity.com says that people need to have 10x of their income at retirement, and it can be achieved if they start saving 15% of their income from age 25 to the retirement age of 67 (*How Much Should I save for Retirement?*). The savings rate is gross (before tax) and includes employee and employer contributions. Of course, that rate increases if you start saving at a later age or want to have more than 80% of your income. Again, the investment company says that if you are in mid 30s, you should have saved 2x your income, 4x by mid 40s, and 7x by mid 50s. Play with retirement calculators that you can easily find online, including one on FINRA.org. First, though, read the following two sections on expected growth and other things to consider.

Be Realistic with Expected Growth

When playing with numbers for your retirement calculation, be careful with an expected average annual return. Historically, the average securities market has gained about 10% annually, although most investors haven't enjoyed those kinds of profits mainly due to investment fees and a lack of diversification. Please understand that the past performance does not guarantee future profits, especially in the era in which low economic growth is expected. For the economy to grow at a fast rate, strong consumer spending, which is about 70% of US GDP, is critical. That means average household income needs to grow at a rapid rate as well. The vast majority of US households has seen their income mostly stagnant or decline over recent decades, while essential family expenses such as education and medical costs increased at a high rate. That has further caused many middle class Americans to not be able to save for their retirement, increasing higher wealth inequality. How we got here and what to do about it is a vital subject to discuss, but it is out of topic for this book. If you're curious, read an insightful article from The New York Times (*We're in a Low-Growth World. How Did We Get Here?*).

My point is that the US economy is expected to grow at a slow rate in the future, therefore, we should expect a lower returns from securities investment, compared to what we have seen in the past. I encourage you to play with different numbers on retirement calculators to see how different expected growth rates can change your plan. If you need to save $300,000 within 15 years and use 10% for expected annual growth, for example, the calculator will tell you that you need to save about $8,600 a year. If you use 5% instead, you'll be required to save over $13,000 a year to have the same $300,000 in 15 years. Big difference, isn't it? Using a high future return will make you feel good now but likely to disappoint you in reality. Many financial advisers use 7% or 8% for expected future returns, but I usually use 6% or 7%. If you are someone who is easily scared by the securities market downturn, then you may need to use a number that is even lower because your portfolio should be invested more conservatively.

As for the inflation rate, mid 3% is a historical average of the past when the economy and the securities market were growing rapidly. I often use a lower inflation rate at around 2%. Again, nobody can tell exactly what future inflation rates and your portfolio growth would be. We are just trying to guesstimate the unknowns, which is why monitoring your plan periodically and modifying it as needed is an integral part of financial planning.

Consider All Possibilities

There are other things that you should consider in retirement planning. For example, if you're married to a much younger spouse, you should plan for a longer retirement duration. With technology advancement, people live longer than ever, so it is highly recommended to plan accordingly, even if you come from a family with a known genetic disease that claimed some family members' lives early. My point here is that you should save more money than you think you need while you can.

You may naturally want to include the equity in your home as your current asset for your retirement planning calculation. While your house may or may not appreciate at a similar rate as diversified securities in the future, the average home price has historically increased at a similar rate as inflation, which is quite lower than the average stock market growth rate. I generally advise people to consider home equity as back up plan and not include it in the calculation to find out how much they should save for their retirement. If you want to include your home equity, do a little research to find out the average home appreciation rate in your area and consider that in your calculation separately from the expected growth rate from securities investment.

Are you expecting a sizable inheritance? Potential inheritance is not your money unless it is in an irrevocable trust (which means that the giver cannot reclaim the assets). It would be wise, in my opinion, not to heavily depend on your potential inheritance for your retirement planning. Even if you are a designated beneficiary of someone's asset or insurance policy, you need to know that the owner may change it at any time. No money is yours until you have it in your name.

Now, please run your numbers to find out how much you need for your retirement and how much you should save each year to reach that goal.

Reduce Expenses

I assume most of you may be devastated wondering how you would ever be able to save what your calculator tells you to save for your retirement. You may be able to save much more than you think by reducing expenses. Suze Orman, a TV star who gives brutally honest financial advice, famously said that young people could save as much as $1 million during their lifetime just by quitting expensive Starbucks coffee. Whether it is realistic or not, she correctly points out the importance and the enormous impact of reducing expenses that so many people don't seem to think matters. Every dollar you spend is a dollar you don't save. So regularly check if there is room to save even on expenses that you may view as fixed.

Review all your monthly expenses such as your phone, cable TV, Internet, utility bills, and insurance premiums on home and auto, not to mention discretionary spending such as lunch and weekend outings. Thanks to increasing competition, companies like phone and TV providers either reduce price or increase services for the same price. Lower the service package if you can, and take advantage of "promotional rates." You may need to call every six months or a year to keep the special rates, but it is worth it.

For home and auto insurance, many companies tend to increase premiums over time even if you don't have any claim. Ask your insurance companies to see if they can lower your premiums for the same coverage, but check other companies anyway. You would be surprised how much you can save on insurance premiums for the same coverage, especially if you have kept the same company for a long time with little or no claims in the past several years. Make sure you have adequate coverage to protect your property, as lower premiums shouldn't come at the expense of inadequate coverage. Increasing the deductible to what you can afford is a good way to reduce insurance premiums. Don't forget to compare life insurance premiums, too. If you have life insurance that is older than 10 years, you may be able to change your current life insurance policy to a new one with the same coverage and lower premiums. That is because, thanks to the Internet, people can compare insurance products and companies are forced to lower premiums to compete.

Compare your mortgage and auto loan interest rates in comparison to what people are currently paying and see if you can save by refinancing the loans. If you plan to sell your home within several years, carefully analyze if you can recoup the refinancing costs through savings in payments in that limited time.

I hope you can reduce your expenses substantially with the "tricks" described above, but all the work of cutting costs means nothing if you don't save the dollars you get to keep. Make sure you increase your retirement savings dollar-for-dollar as soon as you reduce your expenses.

Know Employee Benefits

Too many people focus on the pay rate when getting a new job, ignoring employee benefits. Employee benefits such as a 401(k) match, health insurance, and other benefits can be worth about 30% of total compensation. It means that a job with $70,000 pay and $30,000 worth of benefits is better than a job with $90,000 pay with no benefits, but carefully analyze what the benefit package is worth to *you*. For example, $5,000 for daycare support and another $5,000 for employee education support is not worth anything to you if you don't use them. Remember that you are highly limited in your opportunity to effectively save for their retirement without a group plan, so try to give more weight to one with a 401(k) plan than the one without it. If you're financially savvy and able to save extra, see if the 401(k) plan will allow you to utilize mega backdoor Roth, which is previously explained. If you are not familiar with employer benefits or don't know how to evaluate them, consult a financial planner who's knowledgeable in the topic.

Do I Need a Financial Advisor?

We all have been dealing with our own finances as early as we learned about money. It is easy to think that we know what we need to know regarding personal finances. I grew up poor and learned to be frugal from a very early age. I started working after high school and came to America for school without my parents' help. (However, I had a gracious aunt in America who let me stay in her home for free while I was going to school). I was the first to go to college in my family. Since I worked at a brokerage company in Korea for several years before coming to America, I thought I understood investing. I was so confident that I knew what I needed to know and thought I just had to make "good" money to be financially stable. How naive I was! Being frugal, of course, is essential to achieve financial stability, especially for people like me who don't have rich parents. What I didn't know was that making a good income and being frugal was not enough for me to effectively accumulate and protect my assets. The little knowledge that I obtained working as a clerk at a brokerage company in Korea didn't help me understand securities investment in America.

You can save money in one account that provides tax deductions and deferral of income taxes for decades, while the same amount of money invested in another account may get no such benefits. Assets in one account may be protected from most creditors even in bankruptcy, while the same amount of money in a different account may be vulnerable to all creditors. Unless you extensively studied personal finance, I think you need a financial planner. If I had known what I know now when I got married about 20 years ago, my husband and I would have been in a much better financial situation today with the same income.

Unfortunately, the financial advisory field is like the Wild West, in my opinion, because many "advisors" are mere salespeople without adequate education to provide a holistic financial planning service.

Therefore, finding a qualified financial planner who puts clients' interests above his/her own earnings is a challenge, and it requires a whole chapter. See Chapter 8, Financial Adviser.

Other Things to Consider

The Cruel Reality

When an overwhelming majority of the population is suffering, whether it is from physical, mental, or financial pain, it should be treated as a national crisis like any other disaster that affects the public wellbeing. I'm not sure if most political leaders of the nation who are wealthy know this reality. Do they understand the fear of losing a home or having to choose between paying for medicine and utility bills? Can they really feel the pain of what it is like for parents to hesitate to take a sick child to see a doctor because of a high deductible on health insurance? If they do know, I seriously doubt so many politicians could say and act the way they do today, unless they are a bunch of hypocrites working for their own interests. If these politicians truly care about the people, as they should; they would be sharing the good health care that they enjoy with the people, instead of taking benefits from the sick and old. If they have any idea how frustrated millions of senior Americans are trying to survive day by day, they would be spending time on how to improve Social Security and reduce Medicare costs, instead of trying to give themselves and their rich friends tax cuts so they'd get even richer. We can disagree over many issues, but telling the most vulnerable people in society that they are on their own should not be one of them, especially in the wealthiest nation in the world.

Regardless of differences in political and social views, the brutal reality is that if you don't save today, the quality of your life *can* and *will* get worse. When a tornado is coming, you have to get to safety at all costs because 'too tired' or 'not knowing about the storm' won't save you. Retirement is a perfect storm that is coming to everyone, so we *must* save while we can.

Emotional Beings

With similar income and circumstances, some people financially thrive while others struggle as they get older. Even if they all know how they can improve their finances, many don't act upon it. Why do you think that is? As much as we want to believe that we are rational beings, most of our financial decisions are deeply tied to our emotion, according to the study of behavioral finance. That means knowing what you're supposed to do with your money isn't necessarily getting you financial stability. For me, since I know too well how difficult life can be with little money, I am highly motivated to save. I couldn't care less about what other people think of me with the bags I carry and discount stores I shop. I've never gone to Starbucks for coffee when I can make my own at home. I love my sons dearly, but I won't stop saving for my retirement to send them to college. That is just me, and I understand that different people have different views and priorities, as money decisions are deeply emotional, and there's no one "right" answer. My hope for this section is that, although I share my views, you do soul-searching on your relationship with money and clarify your priorities.

Money and Happiness

They say that money can't buy happiness. I fully understand that there are many things in life that no amount of money can buy, but money certainly *can* solve many problems and make our lives much more enjoyable. I know too well how stressful it can be when one's basic financial needs are not met.

I will never forget the day when I cried over money in 2001. At that time, my husband reduced his hours and income to half from his job while trying to build his own business with a partner. I was a stay home mom with our one-year-old son, and on that day, I was running out of diapers. I opened my wallet to check if I had enough money or a credit card to go to a store for diapers. I found myself looking at several $1 bills, wondering if I could "make" an extra dollar if I were to tear a small portion from each bill and put it all together.

I was born and raised by poor farmers in South Korea. After high school, I had to move to a city to get a job and become financially independent. For about six years, I worked full time and went to English school at night, while saving money to come to America for college. The lack of money never bothered me because I was and still am a very positive person, always looking at the bright side while dreaming and working for a better future. When my husband wanted to start his own business (and reduce his income), I was not at all afraid of supporting him and didn't complain for about two years, although I had to watch my spending down to the pennies. Catching myself thinking of ways to "make" an extra $1 bill, not even a $5 or $10 bill, however, was devastating and broke me down. I never cried over money before or after that day.

'Basic financial needs' are different for individuals and may change depending on situations. For example, you may be relatively happy with $40,000 income right after college living in a city where living expenses are low, or you may feel poor with a $150,000/yr. income if you live in San Francisco with a family because living expenses are very high in that city. Moreover, people are emotional, social beings that consciously and subconsciously compare themselves to others. Even a millionaire may feel poor if surrounded by billionaires, for example. All of these make it very difficult to generalize what we minimally need to be happy. A study by a Princeton University professor, Angus Deaton, suggests in 2010 that $75,000 per year may be used as a benchmark. He says that the less people earn, the more emotional pain they displayed, while making much more than $75,000 doesn't seem to increase the level of happiness significantly. What is your number?

You Now vs. You in the Future

When you think about it, saving for your retirement is you limiting the current joy of spending to save for your future self. Saving the money that you can use for so many things right now is not easy. Your future self will be happy if you save as much as you can now, as I have yet to meet anyone who regrets saving too much while younger. Finding the middle ground both your current and future selves can be happy with is the key.

Someone in her late 60s once told me that an investment adviser told her to start saving $200 a month when she got her first job after college. Retirement sounded too far of a future thing for the 20-something young woman, and she could think of a million better things to do with $200 a month than saving for old age. She ignored the advice. Had she started investing $200 a month for about 45 years, she would've had over $700,000 now, assuming 7% annual compounding. If she could somehow talk to the 45 years younger self, she'd do anything to convince her to save $200 a month, she told me. What would you tell yourself if you could go back 10 years? What do you think yourself in retirement will tell you to do now?

What Does Money Mean to You, Anyway?

Why do you buy what you buy? What does having (wanting) a nice car and a big house mean to you? Why do you care about what other people think of you? Yes, we all like nice things, and we are social beings who cannot be completely free from comparing ourselves to others. And we want our friends and loved ones, especially parents, to be proud of us by showing them how well we live. But at what costs? Are you happy making those payments that you struggle to make every month? One thing that I can tell you with confidence is that those who respect you mainly because of your wealth will not regard you highly once you no longer can afford the lifestyle. They may not even be around you anymore.

My favorite grocery store is Aldi. I love their simple selection of items and, of course, low prices. One day many years ago, I was talking to a small group of housewives, and I mentioned how much I liked Aldi. They looked at me with disappointment, and one even said, "Oh, you shop in *that kind of place*?" And they went on to say why I should buy "quality" products at Whole Foods. I never became good friends with any of them. That is not because their snobbiness bothered me, but because it was painful for me to see them talk as if money is not an issue when I know they mostly lived paycheck-to-paycheck, although their husbands' paychecks may have been quite larger than most people's. I've seen a few of them at Aldi since, and they hurried out as soon as they saw me from a distance.

I don't know if they are happy with the way they live, but I do know that they won't be able to keep shopping at Whole Foods after retirement if they don't save now. Ask yourself questions that only you can answer. Why do you buy what you buy and where you buy? Are you surrounded by people who can positively influence you in general? Will your friends treat you the same way with respect if you no longer can afford your current lifestyle? Are you happy with your finance now? If not, do you want to change for better, and if so, what do you need to do? Through this self-reflecting process, I hope that you'd look at the big picture of your entire life and make financial decisions that you'd be proud of for the rest of your life.

Children Are Not a Retirement Plan

I see many people who think their children would financially support them when they retire. I hope their life will turn out to be as they expect, but I must point out how unrealistic that is.

Both of my parents lived with me in their last years, thanks to my husband's understanding and support of my culture. I grew up in a culture where old parents were expected to live with their children (usually sons) until death. Children were the parents' retirement plan, literally. My parents supported their parents and never saved for their retirement, I mean other than having four children including two sons. I'm grateful that I was able to help my parents, and my children got to live with them. But I must admit that it was quite hard at times to live with my parents, especially after my mother passed away, leaving my stubborn father with an anger issue behind. I now have experienced what it means to take care of old parents financially, mentally, and physically, I cannot ask anyone to do the same for me. I don't know what the future holds, and I may end up depending on my children for survival anyway, but it would be immoral for me not to do my best to avoid it while I can.

If you are thinking of depending on your child(ren) for retirement income, ask yourself this question: Are you currently supporting (or did you support) your parents? If yes, you know how difficult or complicated it is or can be, especially if you're married and have children. If no, how can you expect your children to do what you don't (didn't) or can't do? I understand that even if you put your heart and soul in saving from now on, you may not be able to prepare adequately for a financially independent post-retirement life. That is a reality that most people are living today.

It would be great if your children can help you, but it should never be your "plan" to depend on them. That is not only unrealistic, but it also is a sure way to damage your relationship with your children. Imagine how it would be if your parents expect you to pay for their living expenses until they die. Unless you are wealthy and money is not an object, would you be OK with it? How about your spouse? I don't think so. Then what makes you believe that you can financially rely on your children?

Have a Second Plan

It is not easy to save money, I know. And even if you try very hard, you may not be able to save enough to support your lifestyle after retirement, which may be 20 or 30 years. What can we do now? We need alternative plans. Keep sharpening your skills so you can continue to work as long as you need to. See if you can start a shared living with other people. Learn about a reverse mortgage and search whatever options may be available to you at retirement. The key is to start as soon as you realize you may not have enough retirement funds. If you need help or are not sure, don't hesitate to ask for help from a financial planner. The cost you pay for advice now may save you a great deal of money and anxiety for many years to come.

More Than Money

I want to emphasize that retirement is about more than money. Money is an essential part of life, needless to say, but just because you have enough money at retirement that doesn't mean you will be happy. Think about what retirement means to you. That means many decades of your regularity will go away. You may initially be happy with all the longed-for freedom, but lack of regularity can quickly make you feel bored or lose a sense of purpose. Your grandchildren will grow up quickly and won't need your care for long. Your friends and families may not have money or time to see you as often as you want. Even if they do have enough money and time, they may not want to spend it with you. Sooner or later, you would start losing friends to sickness and death. What would you do then, if you are relatively healthy? Think about your life after retirement long before you get there. Some regularity with human interaction is vital to keep one's mind and body healthy. Find something you like and is beneficial to others. If you enjoy something that you can do by yourself, say painting or writing, maybe you can find a way to teach others. Carefully plan for the new chapter of your life well before you retire.

Chapter 6

EDUCATION PLANNING

It is profoundly challenging for most people to receive a college education without taking student loans because of high costs. Planning early and understanding grants, scholarships, and other financial aids are the key to minimize loans that are a burden to so many Americans, including parents and grandparents.

1. Grants and Scholarships
2. Saving for College
3. Student Loans
4. Education Planning

Chapter 6 | EDUCATION PLANNING

Grants and Scholarships

Grants and scholarships are financial aids that don't need to be repaid, making them the most desirable options for students and parents in general, although opportunities are limited and some may have strings attached. For example, if recipients withdraw early from the program for which they receive a grant or scholarship, they may be liable for repayment. The grant or scholarship amounts may be reduced if circumstances of the recipients change, for instance, if students become part-time from full time or receive other grants or scholarships. The funding comes from the federal and state governments, schools, and other organizations. I'll explain several federal grants that are well known.

Federal Pell Grants

Federal Pell Grants are awarded to undergraduate students who have never earned a bachelor or professional degree. The maximum amount changes yearly, and for 2018-2019 (July 1 – June 30), it is $6,095. Your eligibility depends on several factors such as financial need, education costs, and whether you're a full-time or part-time student. See more information on Federal Pell Grants at StudentAid.ed.gov. (*Federal Pell Grants are usually awarded only to undergraduate students.*)

FSEOG Grant

FSEOG (Federal Supplemental Educational Opportunity Grant) is for undergraduate students with exceptional financial needs. The maximum amount is up to $4,000 per year for 2018-2019, and it needs to be applied for through your school. Unlike a Pell Grant, which all eligible students can receive, FSEOG is limited and on a first come first serve basis. Submitting necessary applications as early as possible is the key to get this grant, assuming eligibility. See more information on FSEOG Grant at StudentAid.ed.gov. (*A Federal Supplemental Educational Opportunity Grant (FSEOG) is a grant for undergraduate students with exceptional financial need.*)

TEACH Grant

TEACH (Teacher Education Assistance for College and Higher Education) grant is provided to students who are willing to work as a teacher in a high-need field in a low-income area for four full academic years. A high-need field is defined as "foreign language, mathematics, reading specialist, science, special education, and any other field that has been identified as high-need by the federal government, state, or a local education agency." Applicants must meet basic federal student aid eligibility and be enrolled in undergraduate or graduate school that participates in the program. The maximum grant amount is $4,000 per year, but due to sequestration, it is reduced by 6.2% (October 1, 2018- September 30, 2019).

Recipients of this grant will have to sign a service agreement that they will fulfill their obligations, per the grant requirements. If service obligations are not met, the grant will become a Direct Unsubsidized Loan and needs to be repaid. The interest accrues from the day the grant is disbursed. Service obligations can be suspended or canceled under certain conditions such as a medical reason or military service. See more information at StudentAid.ed.gov (*A TEACH Grant can help you pay for college if you plan to become a teacher in a high-need field in a low-income area.)*

Iraq and Afghanistan Service Grants

As the name indicates, this grant is for soldiers who were in Iraq or Afghanistan. It also is for people whose parent or guardian died during military service in Iraq or Afghanistan after 9/11, and who are under 24 years of age and enrolled in school at the time of the death of the parent or guardian. The maximum grant is up to $6,095 per year, but because of sequestration, it is reduced by 6.2% (October 1, 2018-September 30, 2019).

Aid for Military Families

There are many financial aid opportunities for current and future military personnel, veterans, and family members. For example, the Army, Air Force, Navy, and Marines each offers ROTC (Reserve Officers' Training Corps) scholarships on various conditions. The VA (Dept. of Veterans Affairs) offers its own financial aid for veterans, widow(er)s, and dependents. Some major organizations with financial aid for military personnel and families are the American Legion, AMVETS, Paralyzed Veterans of America, and Veterans of Foreign Wars. Many other smaller veterans service organizations may offer scholarships for higher education. For more benefits and information, visit StudentAid.ed.gov (*Aid for Military Families*)

How to Find Scholarships

Here are some places that you can look for scholarship opportunities, according to StudentAid.ed.gov (*Find and apply for as many scholarships as you can—it is free money for college or career school!*):

- School counselors from your high school and college
- Search tool from Dept. of Labor on CareerOneStop.org
- Federal agencies on StudentAid.ed.gov
- State grant agency on US Dept. of Education
- Foundations, religious groups, or community organizations
- Professional organizations related to your study
- Your and your parents' employer(s)

Be careful of "service providers" who offer to get your financial help for fees, as they may be scammers. You don't have to pay anything to apply for grants, scholarships, or student loans.

Federal Work-Study Jobs

This program provides students jobs so they can earn money to pay for their education. Undergraduate, graduate and professional students who need financial help can do community service work related to their study. Wages can vary, depending on what you do and if you are undergraduate or graduate student, etc. Schools administer this program and jobs may be on or off campus. Talk to your school's financial aid office to see what's available.

Chapter 6 | EDUCATION PLANNING

Saving for College

There are two major types of education savings accounts that have tax advantages: 529 and Coverdell ESA (Education Savings Account).

Named after the Internal Revenue code and commonly called 529, 529 Education Savings Plans are regulated by states. Contribution deductibility, maximum contribution, investment options, fees, etc., can be different by plans. All monies in 529 accounts grow tax-deferred and are tax-free for qualified withdrawals. There are two types of 529 plans: College Savings Plan that is for any college and the Prepaid College Plan that is for state universities and some private colleges within your state.

529 Prepaid Tuition Plan

As the name implies, the 529 Prepaid Tuition Plan is used to prepay college tuition. You can pay college tuition for your child many years before he/she attends college. The advantage of doing this is that you can lock the college tuition at the time of setting up an account. Let's say you set up an account for your newborn child today. By the time your child is ready to go to college, the tuition may have more than doubled, but you'd pay the lower locked tuition. You can pay in full now or make regular payments over time. Another benefit is that since you're prepaying college tuitions, you don't have to worry about ups and downs of securities markets or investment fees.

There may be restrictions and lack of clarity in prepaid plans, however. If your child ends up going to a school that is not participating in the plan, you'd have to pay its full price tag at the time of admission. You can get your money back from the 529 Prepaid Tuition Plan in that case, but the total return of principal and profits are not likely to be enough to cover tuition for the school your child attends. If you have a younger child, you may be able to change the beneficiary to him/her, but there may be other restrictions. Thus, it is essential that account owners fully understand the rules and restrictions before opening this type of account. For these reasons, straightforward 529 College Savings Plans are more popular.

529 College Savings Plan

Assets in a 529 College Savings Plan can be used for any college and have fewer restrictions, compared to other education savings plans. Again, 529 plans are regulated by states, so your state's program may be different. Contributions may be tax-deductible. Check if your state allows deductions on FinAid.org (*State Tax Deductions for 529 Contributions*). If your state allows a deduction, use the calculator from Vanguard.com to see how much tax your contribution can save you (*529 State Tax Deduction Calculator*). Followings are some general features, as your state plan may differ.

- Can be used for any college and university as well as acceded trade or vocational schools
- Up to $10,000 per year can be used for K-12.
- Monies grow tax-deferred.
- No tax on withdrawals for qualified education (tuition, room and board, school fees, books, etc.)
- High contribution limit: Initial maximum contribution of up to $75,000 without gift tax consequences (2018 & 2019)
- Lifetime maximum contribution differs by states but ranging about

$200,000-$500,000.

- Anyone can contribute with no income limits.
- Multiple accounts can be open for one beneficiary.
- Easy transfer to another beneficiary - No age limits
- Investment controlled by the account owner
- 10% penalty and income taxes on earnings for non-qualified withdrawals with some exceptions
- Direct transfer allowed once every 12 months, not per calendar year

You can open any state's education savings plan(s), but the state income tax deductibility on your contribution may be limited. Pay attention to contribution deductibility, investment options and fees, and other restrictions. Keep the amount that you need in the near future, for example, next year's tuition, in money market funds so it won't be affected in case of market fluctuation when you need the money.

Coverdell ESA

Coverdell Education Savings Account (ESA) is another savings account for education. Some main differences, compared to 529 College Savings Plans, are as follows:

- *K-12 and college*: Coverdell ESAs can be used for grade schools, K-12, as well as college, while 529 is mostly for college and higher education.
- *Low contribution maximum:* The maximum contribution per year is $2,000 per beneficiary, which is significantly less than $15,000 or more in 529 plans. If more than one ESA is open for the same beneficiary, the total contribution from all accounts cannot exceed

the annual limit; otherwise 6% penalty is imposed on the excess contribution. One can open both ESA and 529 accounts for the same beneficiary.

- *No deduction*: Contributions are not tax-deductible, as opposed to many states providing state income tax deduction for 529 contributions.
- *Income limit*: No contribution for those with MAGI (modified adjusted gross income) of $110,000 for singles and $220,000 for joint fillers (2018 & 2019), as opposed to 529 plans with no income restrictions.
- *Beneficiary age limit*: No account can be open or contributions be made on an existing account for a beneficiary 18 or older, unless he/she has special needs.
- *Time limit on distribution:* Assets must be used or transferred by the time the beneficiary is 30, as opposed to 529 savings plans with no age limit.
- *Stock investment*: Individual stock investment is allowed, unlike 529 College Savings accounts that are limited to mutual funds.

For more information on Coverdell ESA, visit IRS.org (*Coverdell Education Savings Account*). For a comparison chart between Coverdell ESA and 529 College Savings Plans, see SavingForCollege.com (*Compare Savings Options*).

Savings Bonds

Another way to save for loved ones' education is by purchasing savings bonds, which used to be popular when interest rates were high. People who don't want any investment risk or responsibility of managing the money prefer savings bonds. Your money is guaranteed by the US government and earns interest. The original investment is not tax deductible, but no income taxes are imposed on the earnings if used for qualified education expenses.

There are two common types of bonds that you can buy for education savings purposes: Series I and Series EE. These savings bonds can be purchased directly from the government website at TreasuryDirect.gov. The maximum purchase amount per person on these two bonds is $10,000 each, with a total of $20,000 per year. Because they are super-safe with the government guarantee, the interest rates on these bonds are super-low: currently at 0.1% per year for Series EE bonds (May 2018). But you get to buy one at a discounted price with a guarantee that the value will double in 20 years. For example, you want to buy a $10,000 Series EE bond; then, you'd pay $5,000, and in 20 years, you'll get $10,000 back. When you consider the interest payments and the doubled price at maturity, you'll earn about 3.5% compounded annually. Series EE bonds can be a good hedge when the economy is expected to grow slowly or contract (recession).

Series I bonds can protect investors in case of high inflation because coupon payments increase with the inflation rate, unlike Series EE bonds with a fixed rate Series. I bonds are currently paying a fixed interest rate of 0.3% and the inflation rate of 2.22%, yielding a total annual rate of 2.52%, as of May 2018.

If you sell your bond within five years of purchase, you lose the last three months of interest payments. The purchase price of these savings bonds are not tax deductible, but if you use the money for education in the year you cash the bond(s), the earnings are not taxed. There is an income

(MAGI) limit for the tax exemption, which is $93,150 for single filers and $147,250 for joint filers (2017). Visit TreasuryDirect.gov for more information on Series EE and Series I savings bonds.

What to Choose for Education Savings

Which education savings method to choose from entirely depends on your circumstances and what you want. If you want a certainty without any investment risk, your options are either 529 Prepaid Tuition Plan or savings bonds. With a prepaid tuition plan, your choice of college is limited, although it won't matter if your child ends up going to one of the schools in the plan. With savings bonds, you are likely to get lower returns than average securities investment, but it may be the only option if you cannot stomach ups and downs of the stock markets and don't want to limit your children's school choice, although there is an income limit for tax deduction on the earnings.

Funds from a Coverdell ESA can be used for all ages from K to college, and you can also invest in a variety of investment options including individual stocks, bonds, and ETFs. In comparison, 529 College Savings Plans are to be used for college and higher education, except for up to $10,000 per year for K-12, and they mostly offer a limited number of mutual funds for investment.

For flexibility and higher savings, you may want a 529 College Savings Plan, especially if your state allows an income tax deduction on the contribution. If your child is close to college age and you don't want to risk losing the principal amount by investing in the securities market, you can invest in money market funds and take advantage of the income tax deduction if available. If you make over $110,000 ($220,000 if married and file tax jointly) or want to save more than $2,000 per year, 529 plans may be your only choice. Of the two 529 plans, if you want to grow your savings and let your child decide later which school she goes to, the 529 College Savings Plan may be your only option.

Student Loans

The best way to pay for college is to receive scholarships and grants, of course, or you can save enough money to pay for college. The reality is that scholarships and grants are limited, and most people are not able to save enough money for college. That is why so many students and parents end up getting student loans. It is important to understand what loans are commonly available and the differences among them.

Student loans, or any loans for that matter, must be paid back, unlike grants and scholarships that don't need to be repaid. Depending on the types, student loans are relatively easier to get. Unlike consumer loans (credit card debt, mortgage, auto loan, etc.), student loans are very difficult (almost impossible) to be forgiven in case of bankruptcy. They can also cause your Social Security benefits to be garnished. Thus, understand the features of any student loans you get and do not borrow more than what you absolutely need.

Federal vs. Private Loans

Student loans can be largely categorized into two types: federal and private loans. Most federal student loans come with better terms, and borrowers need to be within certain income levels. Some of the benefits of federal student loans are, but not limited to, fixed and relatively lower rates, no credit check on borrowers (except for PLUS loan), a generous repayment schedule, and loan forgiveness under certain conditions, etc. It is usually a better idea to seek federal student loans before looking at private loans. Although the federal government is the lender for most student loans, they are administered and disbursed by schools. Your school may not service all federal student loans, so contact your school's financial aid office to find out what's available for you. For a comparison between federal vs. private loans, visit StudentAid.ed.gov. *(What are the differences between federal and private student loans?)* I mostly discuss federal student loans in this section.

Federal Perkins Loans

Perkins Loans are a federally funded student loan program with a low-interest rate at 5% and generous repayment conditions. It is designed to help students and families with exceptional financial needs. As of 2018, however, the loan is no longer available, so I'll not further discuss it here. If you already have obtained this loan and are still in school, you can start making payments nine months after you leave school or drop below half-time status.

Direct Subsidized Loans

Direct Loans (also known as Stafford Loans) are federally funded student loans as well, and there are two types: subsidized and unsubsidized. Like Perkins Loans, Direct Subsidized Loans are designed to help students with a low income; therefore, you must demonstrate financial need to obtain this loan. The allowable income range is wider than Perkins Loans, and your school decides on the eligibility and amount of the loan. Direct Subsidized Loans are only for undergraduate students.

Students with this loan don't need to make interest payments while enrolled, and the grace period before having to make interest plus principal payments is *six months* after graduation.

The interest rate for Direct Subsidized loans is 5.05%, and there is an origination fee of a little over 1%, which is deducted at the time of fund disbursement (July 2018 - June 2019). No credit check is required. The maximum amount for Direct Subsidized Loans is $5,500-$12,500 per year, depending on needs, years in school, and other financial aid received. FAFSA must be updated each year to get these loans.

Direct Unsubsidized Loans

The most significant difference between Direct Subsidized Loans and Direct Unsubsidized Loans, other than Direct Subsidized is only for undergraduates, is who pays the interest payments while students are enrolled in school: the federal government or the student borrowers. For Direct Subsidized Loans, the federal government makes the interest payments until six months after students finish or terminate education. For Direct Unsubsidized Loans, borrowers are responsible for interest payments once the loans are obtained, though they can be deferred until graduation. Recurring interest payments will be added to the principal amount if deferred.

The interest rate for undergraduate students is the same as Direct Subsidized Loans at 5.05%, but it is 6.6% for graduate and professional students (July 2018 - June 2019). The loan fee is about 1.06%, and borrowers can choose repayment options between 10 to 25 years.

For undergraduate students, the maximum Direct Unsubsidized Loan amount is $5,500-$12,500 per year, depending on the year in school, whether they are dependent or not for their tax filing status, and whether their parents are able to get a Plus loan or not. The aggregate limit for both Direct Subsidized and Unsubsidized loans is $31,000-$57,500 for undergraduate students, depending on the conditions described above.

Graduate students and professional students can borrow up to $20,500 per year. Their aggregate total amount for both Direct Subsidized and Unsubsidized Loans is $138,500, including all federal loans for undergraduate study. For more information on Direct Subsidized Loans and Direct Unsubsidized Loans, visit StudentAid.ed.gov (*Subsidized and Unsubsidized Loans*). As stated earlier, schools manage these loans, so the best way to find out what's available for you is by talking to the financial aid office of the school you (plan to) attend.

Direct Plus Loans

Federally funded Direct Plus Loans are available for graduate or professional students and parents of dependent undergraduate students. Like other federal student aid programs, this too is made through participating schools. Unlike other federal student loan programs, borrowers need to have good credit to be qualified for Direct Plus Loans. If you have an adverse credit history, you can either have an endorser (co-signer) with good credit or successfully appeal to the US Department of Education. The interest rate is fixed at 7.6% for disbursements between July 2018 and June 2019. The maximum loan amount is generous in this loan, which is the total education costs (determined by the school) minus other financial aid. The loan fee is much higher than other federal loans at about 4.25%, which is deducted at the time of loan disbursement (October 2018-September 2019). Borrowers can decide the repayment term between 10-25 years.

If you are a student with this loan, you can defer payments until six months after graduation or leaving the school. If you are a parent, you also can postpone making payments until your child finishes, but I strongly recommend you start making payments without any delay. Though this loan is for your child, it is in your name, and you are solely responsible for the entire debt, even if your child never earns any income from the education. You cannot transfer this loan to your child's name later, either. Besides, deferring payments only increase your later payments because the interest payments start accruing after the loan is disbursed. As I repeat throughout the book, student loans will seldom be dismissed even through bankruptcy and can garnish your Social Security checks. Thus borrow the very minimum amount necessary and start making payments as soon as you get a loan. See more information on Plus Loans on StudentAid.ed.gov.

Other

There are need-based, competitive student loans for health professions students from the Department of Health Resources and Services Administration (HRSA). They are designed to encourage more students to be health professionals because America needs a lot more of them than it is currently producing. There are five loan programs offered: Loans for Disadvantaged Students (LDS), Health Professional Student Loans (HPSL), Primary Care Loans (PCL), Nursing Student Loans (NSL), and

Nurse Facility Loan Program (NFLP). Like other federal student loan programs, they are school-based programs, so talk to the school financial aid office of the school you (will) attend for more information. The department also offers grants and scholarships. See more information on financial aid from the Department of Health and Human Services on HRSA.gov (*School-Based Scholarships and Loans*).

Don't forget to look at your state government for any financial aid available. In Missouri, for example, students with 31 or higher on ACT scores may receive an academic scholarship of up to $3,000 if they go to school in the state.

Ways to Pay for College

As a general rule of a preferred way to pay for college, grants and scholarships are the first. Work-Study Jobs also should be considered if possible. Your savings come next, leaving loans as the last option. Among loans, Direct Subsidized Loans, Direct Unsubsidized Loans, and Direct Plus Loans should be considered in that order for preferable rates and conditions. Federal student loans may be limited in availability, which is why you should apply as soon as possible.

For many students, whatever grants, scholarships, and federal student loans, including savings and any money they can earn from part-time work, may still not be enough to cover total education costs. Private student loans can fill the gap, but their eligibility requirements are stricter, and interest rates tend to be higher, so please consider private student loans as the last resource. For those parents with excellent credit history and financial ability to repay, however, private loans *may* be a better choice than a Plus loan. Eligibility and amounts for private student loans are based on one's personal credit rating and financial ability to repay, like any other consumer loans. There are specialized private loans for professional students such as medical students and law school students. Visit FinAid.org (*Private Student Loans*) and NerdWallet.com (*Private Student Loans: 6 Best Lenders for 2018*) for some private student loans comparison and other useful information.

Many parents take an equity loan from their home because equity loans usually have lower rates than private student loans. That decision should be made with careful consideration. Consult a financial professional who is a fiduciary before increasing your own debt for your children's education. Even if you end up taking an equity loan for your children's college, you should fully understand how it can affect the rest of your life, especially your retirement planning.

FAFSA

Free Application for Federal Student Aid (FAFSA) is a form that is required to be considered for federal student grants, scholarships, and loans. As an independent student or a parent of a dependent student, you will need to disclose your income and assets in detail, including your tax filing information. Once you complete FAFSA, you'll know how much financial aid you are eligible for and how much your expected family contribution (EFC) is. The numbers are estimates only and can change depending on the school you (your child) attend. Many private colleges and universities require an additional financial form called CSS Profile. I've seen families who don't bother with FAFSA, assuming that they may not be eligible for federal student aid due to their higher than average income. Filling out FAFSA and updating it each year can be cumbersome and time-consuming, I know. But I highly recommend you fill it out as you (your child) apply for college if you need *any* financial help, including loans. At the very least, check out the school's Net Price Calculator (NPC) before giving up on FAFSA. It is a great way to check if you may be able to get any financial aid from the school of your interest, and it only takes a few minutes.

High school seniors can file FAFSA from early October. If you have any question or see a section that does not apply to you and the online FAFSA application doesn't let you skip it, contact FAFSA's customer service. Your school also may accept a paper form.

Only US citizens and permanent residents (also called green card holders) are eligible for federal student aid, but private colleges often have their own extra set of rules for financial aid that are usually more generous than federal rules. The best way to find information on available financial assistance for all students, including international students, is by contacting the financial aid office of your school.

Education Planning

Understand the Costs

Understanding costs of college is the first step in education planning. According to College Board (CollegeBoard.org), the average total costs for public in-state four-year institutions for the 2018-2019 academic year is $25,890 ($41,950 for out-of-state students), and $52,500 for private non-profit institutions, including room and board (*Average Estimated Undergraduate Budgets, 2018-2019*). Most well known private universities have a $60,000-$70,000 price tag, though they tend to provide more generous financial aid. Use Net Price Calculator for the school of your interest to estimate how much you are expected to pay.

Historically, college costs have risen at a much higher rate than average inflation. If you (your children) have many years before having to pay for college, consider this in your education planning, meaning you need to save much more than what you think you need today.

Start Saving at Birth and Ask Families to Help

Considering enormous costs, it is never too early to start saving for your children's college education. I strongly recommend opening an education account right after your child's birth. Technology makes it very easy for anyone to contribute into your education savings account these days. Ask your friends and families to help save for your child's education, instead of buying gifts.

There are too many children who get gifts that are worth hundreds of dollars for birthdays and holidays each year, but they have no college savings account. It is sad and wrong for many reasons. What are we teaching our children by buying things that are likely to get lost or thrown away soon or later, when we know there are no savings for their education? We all have been in a situation where we wonder if whatever we buy for others is a good gift. We also have been in a situation thinking whatever we did get from others was a waste of money and wished we got cash instead. Haven't you? I have. Then why don't we fix it by helping each other with our children's education savings? You may not feel comfortable asking people what to do with their money, but you *can* offer to help with their college savings instead of buying gifts. Hopefully, they will get the memo and do the same for you. Your contribution of $20 or $30 may not sound like much, but aggregate amounts can be substantial. For example, if 10 people each contribute $25 (a total of $50 per person per year) for your child's birthday and Christmas or whatever holiday you celebrate, there will be over $16,000 available for education after 18 years, assuming 6% compound interest. If you, the parent, also contribute $50 a month from your child's birth, there will be over $36,000 by the time your child is ready for college. It may not be enough to cover all education costs for him/her, but it certainly will help. Creating or changing that "culture" around you can take courage, but that is one way you can financially help yourself and others with the money you're spending anyway.

Talk to Your Child

I understand that many teenagers want to go to school far from their parents. But going to a school out of state can be a very costly proposition and set you (and your child) in debt for decades to come. If you are a parent, talk to your child and help him/her understand the costs and the reality. College planning must include everyone that is involved, especially if student loans are needed. Student loans are considered to be good debts, but they can bite you harder than other consumer loans, as explained throughout the book. If you don't include your child in his/her college planning, you are missing an opportunity to teach a critical life lesson. Do not pretend that things will be paid somehow. Not letting your children know of the reality of debts, especially if they have to get student loans in their name, is irresponsible and dangerous, in my opinion. Be honest and start talking as early as possible. They'd understand more than you think. If you are a teenager not yet in college, ask your parents how your education costs will be paid.

Major Matters

It is ideal to do what you are passionate about and make enough money to support yourself. The reality is that not all college degrees are in demand by organizations that can pay you enough to live independently. Many people with an expensive college degree are struggling to find a job that matches their area of study. Unless you are from a wealthy family and never need to worry about paying for college, be realistic in choosing a major. I'm not saying you should study engineering just because it is one of the majors that can land you a good job when you have no interest in that field. I don't think you should give up your dream because you're afraid of job prospects, either. The inarguable fact is that we all need money to be able to do what we love in life. Thus, fully understand what you can do with the degree you want to get upon graduation. If you want to study something that is not likely to land you a job with a living wage you need, consider double majoring or minoring in something that increases the job prospect. If you are constantly worried about making payments such as rent and other bills, it is very difficult, if not impossible, to pursue your dream for long. I would much rather you take a detour toward making your dream come true later than being forced to give that up for financial reasons.

Someone that I know always wanted to be an actress as far back as she remembered. She also knew how difficult it would be to "make it," so she studied education instead. While working as an educator, she helped students and community residents after school and on weekends to produce a play and perform it. She recently retired, and when I saw her last, she was busy planning playgroup(s) of senior citizens with an ambition to perform all over the country. I don't know if she will make her dream come true, but I do know that she will be able to do what she's most passionate about for the rest of her life without worrying about basic living expenses. I sincerely hope that you'd live a life doing what you love, but it requires balancing your dream and reality. Please do not put yourself in a position of having a college diploma and no or little income, while student loans suffocate you.

Don't Forget Community College

Attending a local community college is an inexpensive way to obtain education for under $5,000 per year, according to CommunityCollegeReview.com (*Average Community College Tuition Cost 2018-2019*). They offer a vast number of associate degrees that can help you get a job upon graduation. Many states provide ways for high school students to attend local community college for free by participating in community service and maintaining a certain level of GPA throughout high school. Even for students who want to get a higher education, they can take many general education courses and later transfer them to a four-year college, saving a great deal of money.

When I decided to go back to school to study finance many years ago, I first took classes at a local community college that were accepted by the state university toward my degree. I was able to save over $10,000 by doing it. I understand that it is not considered "cool" for high school graduates to go to a local community college, but getting a degree with less money is way cooler, in my view. Unless you can pay for a university education without loans, take a moment (with your child) and compare the costs of taking classes at a local community college.

Chapter 6 | EDUCATION PLANNING

Maximizing Financial Aid

Different schools have different financial aid packages, and they have discretion on who gets what. You should start talking to people at the financial aid office at the school you plan to attend as early as possible. High school seniors and parents can fill out FAFSA from early October and consult their school counselor regarding financial aid. If there's any change, such as job loss after the submission of the FAFSA, quickly update it and contact the school(s) to seek more help. The less assets you have, the more likely you/your child will get more financial aid. The same amount of assets may or may not affect expected family contribution (EFC), depending on where they are. For example, the equity in your home and money in your retirement accounts don't generally affect how much financial aid you/your child gets in FAFSA. Even for the same small business you own, depending on the entity, you may be able to adjust your income, thereby maximizing potential financial aid. Like any other planning, optimal education planning takes time, often many years. I recommend you start planning with a professional as soon as possible.

Care for Going Abroad?

As you know, college education costs a lot of money in America, but that is not true for the rest of the developed countries in the world. Many western European countries have free or low tuition colleges, even for international students. They offer the same benefits to international students to attract smart people from all over the globe and to allow their young citizens to experience the diversity of culture. Many offer classes in English, so if you are interested in a little adventure, why not look outside of the box?

Other Things to Consider

People tend to favor well-known schools when applying for college, and I fully understand the social implications of being associated with prestigious schools. These famous schools are usually expensive private universities. They attract smart students from all over the world, and many of them are from very wealthy families. I often hear that students who grew up in a comfortable middle-class household suddenly feel poor surrounded by many "rich students" in private universities. If you haven't established a healthy concept of money and wealth, you would feel very poor amongst people with much more money than you and your family have. That can have more damaging effects on young adults than the overall benefits of going to a top-notch university.

Another thing that you should consider is whether you want to be a big fish in a small pond or a small fish in a big pond, as my favorite author Malcolm Gladwell puts it in his book, *David and Goliath*. This question is related to the previous money topic and self-perception. We human beings have a strong tendency to compare ourselves to others around us. That is why famously smart students in their schools can suddenly feel "stupid" and lose self-confidence in a university with elites from around the world. Prestigious universities provide many opportunities that may not be available in other places, but only a small number of people excel in any organization. You need to understand how you may feel if you suddenly are mediocre in a famous university instead of a superstar that you had been in your local high school. Malcolm

Gladwell concludes that being a big fish with confidence in a small pond is better than barely treading as a small fish in a big pond. I highly recommend reading his book, *David and Goliath*. You can get a glimpse of the book in an article on Business Insider (*Malcolm Gladwell's Fascinating Theory On Why You Should Be A Big Fish In A Little Pond*).

Finally, understand that college is not for everyone. We are living in a society where too many people think higher education equals good jobs. While people with higher educations tend to make higher wages in general, it is also true that many highly educated people cannot find a job in their field of study or don't get paid enough to justify the costs and time spent on their higher education. I've met many people with a master's or doctorate who cannot find a job because their study is highly specific and there aren't enough positions available nationwide. Before you (or your child) apply for a college, ask yourself how the college education can help you have a better life. If you (or your child) are not sure, search for alternatives. Many well-paying professional jobs don't require a college education. IT workers, air traffic controllers, construction managers are some professional jobs that pay high salary but don't require college degrees (MoneyCrasher.com – *11 High Paying Six-figure Jobs Without a College Degree*). Vocational schools or community college programs that are designed to train workers may get you much farther than many four-year college degrees, financially speaking. There are even some companies with an apprenticeship where new employees fresh out of high school get paid while learning the necessary skills on the job. Besides, you can go (back) to school anytime, once you find out how a college education can help you. Live smart.

Chapter 7
INVESTMENT

All investment has risks, but most people who have to work for a living cannot afford not to invest because their cash savings will lose values to inflation over time. Understanding investment risks, options, and costs are critical in successful investment.

1. Why Invest?
2. Securities and Index
3. Investment Costs
4. How to Start Securities Investment

Why invest?

Your Money Loses Its Value if Not Invested

Many people are afraid of investing, and I fully understand the fear of losing their hard-earned money. The idea of losing any money especially when so many of us are barely making ends meet is terrifying. The problem with not investing, however, is that it is a guaranteed way of losing your money's value to inflation, a loss of purchasing power. Look up or think about how much things used to cost: average income, costs of food, personal service like haircut and lawn service, housing, etc. Prices of goods and services increase over time, meaning you need to pay more dollars to buy the same things as time goes by. So if your money doesn't minimally "grow" at the inflation rate, your money loses its purchasing power.

In 1970, the average annual household income was about $10,000, according to Census data (*Historical Income Tables: Households*). That means that an average family was able to live on $10,000 a year at that time. Imagine that in 1970, your grandfather who was afraid of losing in investments saved $10,000 in a bank safety box for his retirement. Fast forward to the year 2015, where an average household income is about $57,000 (Census). What do you think he can buy with that money? Only $10,000 worth of goods and services, right? That is about 18% of what he could buy back in 1970. His money lost 82% of its value over 45 years! Had the money been invested in S&P 500 index funds instead, it would have grown over $200,000 during the same period (S&P 500 Index increased to 2,000 in 2015 from about 90 in 1970), without considering investment costs. I cannot stress enough how important it is for people to understand how inflation weakens your cash value. Simply put, most of us cannot afford to keep our savings in "safe" cash because consequences of not investing are much worse over a long period. Unless you are extremely wealthy, you must save, and your money has to grow for you to continue the lifestyle you are used to after retirement.

Time = Money

Try to solve this quiz:

You and your friend are the same age and have the same amount of income. You start saving $5,000 per year from now for the next 10 years and earn 8% annually on your investments that are reinvested. After the 10th year, you stop saving for some reason and just let the money grow at the same annual 8% that is reinvested. However, your friend doesn't save anything for the first 10 years while you're saving, but from the 11th year, he starts saving $5,000 per year and earns the same 8% annual return that is reinvested. Please take a moment to fully understand the situation: The annual savings of $5,000 and the 8% return are the same for both of you. The only difference is that you saved for the first 10 years and stopped, while your friend started his savings from the 11th year. Now, here's the question: for how long do you think your friend has to keep saving $5,000 per year to catch up to you? Take a wild guess: 10, 20, or 30 years?

The answer is *never*. Although you saved only for 10 years, your friend can never catch up to your investment assets even if he keeps saving $5,000 every year forever, getting the same annual return as you

Chapter 7 | INVESTMENT

do. Why? That is because of this little "magic" called compound interest and time. See the chart below.

Years	You		Your Friend	
	Principal	Assets	Principal	Assets
10	$50,000	$78,227	$0	$0
20	50,000	168,887	50,000	78,227
30	50,000	364,615	100,000	247,115
50	50,000	1,699,454	200,000	1,398,905
70	50,000	7,912,081	300,000	6,767,352
100	$50,000	$79,707,116	$450,000	$68,709,269

When you save $5,000 at the beginning of the first year and earn 8% ($400), your money will grow to $5,400 at the end of the year. At the beginning of the 2nd year, you'd save $5,000 again, making the total be $10,400. By the end of the second year with another 8% return, you'd have $11,232. On the first day of the 3rd year, you'd save $5,000, increasing your total to $16,232. And by the end of that year, you'd earn another 8%, increasing your balance to $17,531, and so on. When you keep doing it every year, you'd have $78,227 by the end of the 10th year. Although you don't save anything on the 11th year, the 8% return alone would increase your total assets by $6,258. That is more than what your friend would get by the end the first year of saving plus profit, which is $5,400. From that moment, your 8% yearly return will always be more than what your friend saves plus his returns. That is why your friend will never be able to catch you up even if he keeps saving $5,000 every year for 100 years, as you can see on the table. It is the price of waiting for 10 years that your friend has to pay.

Of course, continuous annual 8% profit is difficult to realize, especially in the economy that is expected to grow slowly in the years to come. This example is to show how compound interest and time can do the magic. Time *is* money.

Understanding Investment Risks

Yes, investment comes with risk, and you can lose all or most of what you invest. But what is a risk, anyway? When you think about it, everything we do has potential risks. Driving to work has a risk of getting into an accident. Many of us know or know of at least one person who got killed or seriously injured in a car accident. Even food can make you sick. We often hear a food poisoning alert and a recall of grocery items. Medicine can cause serious side effects, too. What happens if we do not go to work or eat because of potential risk or skip necessary medication to avoid side effects? Our survival is at risk then, right? The consequences of not doing what's needed to survive are worse than potential risks. Therefore, we *manage* those potential risks by driving carefully, avoiding food that may make us sick, and by carefully monitoring health with a doctor. Assuming we agree that investment is necessary to protect the value of our hard-earned money, all we can do is to manage potential investment risk.

Let's talk about investment risk now. What do you think about investing all your money in one company's stocks? No matter how well any given company is doing right now, there's no guarantee that it would continue to prosper in 20 or 30 years, not to mention a longer time. Thus, investing in one company is said to be highly risky. How about investing equally among five companies? Is it as risky? It depends, but generally speaking, it is very risky for the same reason of uncertainty that the future holds. Most people who say the stock market is too dangerous are those who (or know of others who) invested in a few stocks or didn't prepare for ups and downs of the market and lost big. I know someone who invested heavily in his company's stocks for a few decades only to see his company (and his money) vanish in front of his eyes, as he was getting ready to retire. He never thought that his company, a multinational corporation, would go out of business in his lifetime.

How about investing in established 30 large companies in different industries? The chance of all 30 companies in various sectors going down in the future seems much lower than one or five companies going bankrupt, doesn't it? Statistically speaking, it is much less risky to invest in 30 companies than in a few. Then how about investing in 500 leading US companies in all different sectors? What's the likelihood of all of those companies going bankrupt? Again, nobody knows for sure, but it seems highly unlikely, statistically speaking, doesn't it?

Of course, stock markets go up and down. Remember the worst financial crisis since the Great Depression in US history? During late 2008 to early 2009, the S&P 500, which is an index that tracks stock prices of 500 large US companies in all economic sectors, went down about 50%. There were three groups of people who reacted to that turmoil. The first group was those who were worried about a further market fall and cashed out. The second group was people who understood that the market fluctuated and held tight. The last group was those who saw a once in a lifetime opportunity and invested more money in the market. Can you guess who the winners are 10 years after the market chaos? Those who viewed the market crash as a buying opportunity and invested with diversification at the bottom have quadrupled their money. The market recovered within about four years from the lowest point and doubled after that. Investors who held tight also were rewarded for their patience. Those who couldn't hold tight and left the market lost a significant portion of their money forever. You can imagine what they must be saying about investing in securities and how risky it is.

Ever since the birth of the New York Stock Exchange in the late 1770's, the grand upward trend of the stock markets has been made of many ups and downs. We cannot foresee the future, so all we can do is to learn from the past and prepare for many scenarios. If we know that the securities market fluctuates, an occasional downturn won't be a surprise. If we invest in 500 large companies or even more, we wouldn't need to panic if a few go bankrupt. If we understand that a stock market can crash as it did in 2008-2009, then such turmoil can be viewed as a great buying opportunity rather than a time to panic. If you expect to retire in the relatively near future, say within five years, it would make a lot of sense to keep some of the money in cash or cash-equivalent investment so your cash flow won't be affected much even if the market goes down and takes years to recover, wouldn't it? We may not be able to prepare for all future investment risks, but we sure can minimize potential risks by understanding and planning for them. When investing is not an option to protect the value of our hard-earned money and grow it, just like eating is not an option for our survival, understanding and managing potential risks is all we can do, in my view.

Chapter 7 | INVESTMENT

Securities vs. Real Estate investment

Before I go further, I want to discuss real estate investment because I meet many people who compare it to securities investment and argue real estate is a better way to accumulate assets. I cannot definitively say one is better than the other because it depends on many circumstances, but the average historical appreciation rate on real estate market in the US has been lower than the return of the securities market. For example, Forbes.com reported that during 1990-2005, the average home prices rose 247%, which is a lot. The S&P 500 Index, on the other hand, gained over 1,000% during the same period (*Real Estate vs. Stocks*).

Buying, renting out, and selling a piece of real estate may seem easy to understand compared to what's involved in securities investment. The fact that you can see your investment with your own eyes, whether it is a piece of land or a rental property, can give you a sense of security, but I want to point out that real estate investment is quite risky by definition because you invest a large sum of money in one piece of real estate. It is somewhat like investing in only one company's stocks. Moreover, it is not easy to liquidate, meaning you cannot sell it quickly as you can with securities. Many small real estate investors lose their properties due to this illiquidity problem when the economy is bad. Since most of their money is tied to real estate properties that cannot be easily or partially sold, negative cash flows can quickly put them in a loan payment delinquency. In that situation, the owners may not be able to borrow more money against their properties or refinance the loan because their properties are likely to be appraised lower than they were during good economic conditions. With a lack of cash, the owners will have to sell their property at a much lower price or follow a foreclosure procedure, both of which will cause a significant loss.

Even if small real estate investors can avoid the above situation, potential vacancy and ongoing expenses, including taxes, insurance, community fees, and repairs can quickly add up to total investment costs. If you have tenants who don't or cannot make payments on time, things become complicated. Evicting tenants is a stressful and lengthy legal process, not to mention your loss of income for months or possibly years. If you hire a company to manage your property, it costs about 10% of your monthly rent. Even if your rental property generates income with no problem, it is taxed as ordinary income, which is a higher rate than capital gains tax that you'd pay in dividends from long-term securities investment.

As previously stated, I cannot say one is undoubtedly a better way to invest your money than the other because many things can affect the results. It also depends on your personality and skill set. But it is difficult for me, a landlord of 10 plus years and a registered securities investment adviser, to argue for real estate investment over securities investment. That is because I find securities investment much easier and more rewarding. Financial reward becomes even better if invested in retirement accounts, which offer excellent tax benefits and protection from general creditors that are not offered in real estate investment. Before you decide between securities and real estate investment, consult your financial planner and tax adviser who are knowledgeable in both areas.

Chapter 7 | INVESTMENT

Securities and Index

Definition of Securities

A security represents any ownership that has a financial value that can be traded. Examples of a security can be broad, including but not limited to, business partnerships, stocks, bonds, funds, options, futures, farm animals, and oil and other mineral rights. I will mainly focus on several types of securities that can easily be bought and sold by individuals at a market: bonds, stocks, mutual funds, and ETFs. I explain basics of these types of securities without getting into much detail. If you want to learn more about securities, getting a book(s) may be the best way. If you rather do it online for "free," be careful of your sources, as you can easily fall for websites that are designed to lure investors to buy particular securities. I think Investor.gov is a good place to start, as it is designed for educational purposes by the US Securities and Exchange Commission (SEC) for individual investors.

Bonds

You Lend Money and Receive Interest Payments
Bonds are issued by organizations (issuers) to borrow money from investors, and in return, the issuers pay investors periodic interest payments. Bonds are called debt securities because issuers must pay back the principal with interest to the investors, just like any consumer debt that needs to be paid back to the lender. Some bonds don't pay any interest (they are called zero-coupon bonds), but at the end of the debt term called maturity, investors get the principal plus premium.

When you invest in a bond, you receive fixed interest payments called coupons typically twice a year, and at maturity, you receive the initial investment amount called face value. For a simple example, say you invest $10,000 in a 10-year corporate bond that pays 5% annual interest (coupon). Then you'd receive $500 each year, and at the end of the 10th year, you'd get your $10,000 back.

Bonds can be issued by any organization such as local or federal governments, schools, hospitals, and for-profit companies. Interest payments (coupons) are lower for highly rated bonds because they are considered safer than those with lower credit ratings. Hence, bonds with lower ratings typically pay higher interest rates to compensate investors for the higher risk that they are taking. Bonds with a longer maturity tend to have higher interest rates than those with a shorter maturity, even if the same organization issued them. In case of an organization's bankruptcy and liquidation, bond investors, who are lenders, are ranked higher for their right to claim their assets over stock investors, who are owners of the organization.

Inflation Risk

The features of a regular interest income and the return of original investment at maturity are two of the main reasons many retirees and conservative investors prefer bond investment. While these features may provide peace of mind to investors, however, they can face another type of risk: inflation risk. In other words, because interest payments and the initial investment amount (face value) don't grow, both interest earnings and your principal amount could lose value over time. That is why bonds with longer terms usually pay higher interest rates to compensate for this risk, but the face value never changes. In times of expected economic downfall, bond investment can be a good hedge against market risk, but in times of healthy growing economy, it can face inflation risk or limited asset growth.

If You Want to Trade Bonds Before Maturity

Bonds can be bought and sold at the bond market, but you may or may not get the full price for what you paid for if you want to sell it before its maturity. In times when interest rates are increasing, compared to when you purchased the bond, your bond price will be lower. Think about it: if your bond pays less money than the market average, who would want to buy it when other bonds with higher payments are available? That is why you need to compromise by lowering your bond price if you want to sell it. In times of decreasing interest rates, if your bond pays higher payments than other bonds, more people would want yours, which increases the market price of your bond. In either case, as a bond gets closer to the maturity, its market price gets closer to the face value ($1,000 in most cases).

Some common types of bonds are corporate bonds issued by companies, T-bonds issued by the US Treasury, municipal bonds issued by local governments and municipalities, and school bonds.

Stocks

You Buy Ownership

Stocks represent ownership of an organization. When you buy common stocks of a company, say Microsoft, you buy a piece of ownership of that company. As a part owner of the company, which is called a shareholder, you have a right to vote on some issues such as the executive officers' compensation packages and a proposed merger.

Investment Values Increase If Companies Do Well

As the company grows, the value of your stocks increases, and the company may also pay shareholders dividends. If the company doesn't do well, however, your share price will go down. If the company were to go out of business, you are likely to lose most or all of your investment. Since you are a shareholder (owner), not a bondholder (creditor), the company is not obligated to pay you periodic fixed interest payments. Even dividend payments are discretionary. One of the main reasons that investors buy stocks instead of bonds is because stocks tend to have a lower inflation risk because they *can* grow in value as the company does well over time. In comparison, a bond price at its maturity doesn't increase, no matter how well the bond issuer does.

Preferred stocks have characteristics of both debt securities and equity securities because they pay dividends somewhat like coupons in bonds, but they are stocks whose prices can grow. Preferred stock investors don't have the same voting right as common stockholders do, and their right for the asset in case of the organization' liquidation process is ranked lower than the bondholders'.

How Stock Prices are Determined

People tend to think shares with high prices are more valuable, but that is not necessarily true. When it comes to a price of stocks, think of it as a pie. If you cut a big pie in 100 pieces, each piece will be much smaller than if you cut it in 10 pieces, right? Initial stock prices are determined the same way. For example, say a company is raising capital of $1 million by selling common stocks. If it issues 100 shares, the initial stock price will be $1,000, whereas if it issues 1 million shares, the price per share is $1.

Once shares are issued and freely traded in the market, their prices are determined by many factors such as the company's earnings, the potential, and the economic outlook, etc. If investors view a company with high potential, the price of the company's shares can rise even if the company's not currently profitable. Share prices of highly profitable companies with no known problems can still go down if there is a market risk such as economic turmoil or national security risks.

As companies grow, their stock price will naturally increase as well. Companies can artificially keep their stock price in a range and control it by splitting or reverse-splitting. Let's say that the price of ABC Inc. shares is $100, and the company wants to keep the price at around $50 to appeal to small investors, for example. Then, ABC Inc. can do a 2-for-1 split. After the split, investors will have twice as many shares at half price, but their total investment value remains the same. If you had 100 shares of ABC Inc. at $100 before the split, you'd end up with 200 shares at $50 each afterward.

Companies that want to increase the share price can do a reverse-split. In a 1-for-2 reverse split, investors will end up with a half number of shares at a doubled price. In the previous example, you'd end up with 50 shares at $200 each after a 1-for-2 reverse-split. Your total value of $10,000 isn't affected by either split. A company may choose to increase the stock price by reverse-splitting to boost its image to attract more investors or prevent the shares from being delisted in the stock exchange.

Common Ways to Categorize Stocks

Other than by industry, there are several common ways to categorize stocks:

Small Caps are stocks with a lower total market value, called market capitalization, between approximately $300 million and $2 billion. Market capitalization, which is calculated by multiplying outstanding shares and the market price per share, can frequently change as stock prices change. Some "hidden gems" may be found more often in this category than larger companies because these small companies are often not known to many investors. For the same reason, the risk may be high as well.

Mid Caps are stocks with a medium market capitalization of approximately $2 billion to $10 billion.

Large Caps have over $10 billion in market capitalization.

Blue-Chip stocks are shares of large and well-established companies with steady growth and often with less volatility than other stocks. Most blue-chip stocks tend to be top leaders in their industry and move closely with Dow Jones Industrial Average and S&P 500 Index. The name comes from poker game where blue chips have the highest value.

Income Stocks pay dividends almost like interest payments (coupons) in bonds, though companies are not obligated to pay dividends to common stock shareholders, while coupon payments in bonds are legal obligations. Unlike coupons in bonds, which are fixed until maturity, dividends of income stocks can grow over time. Shares of utility companies and matured consumer product companies such as Johnson & Johnson and Coca-Cola are examples in this group. Investors who want both income and growth often invest in income stocks. These stocks tend to be less volatile than the market, meaning their prices are more stable, compared to other stocks. That is because we all need electricity, shampoo, food, drinks, etc., regardless of the ups and downs of the stock market or economy.

Value Stocks are believed to be priced lower than their actual or potential value. They tend to have a low price-to-book (P/B) value or price-to-earnings (P/E) ratio. They may pay dividends. Shares of stable companies that are experiencing unexpected price decline due to bad publicity or lawsuit may be viewed as value stocks. Investors who expect a foreseeable future price increase with maybe some dividends along the way tend to buy these securities.

Growth Stocks are shares of companies that tend to be newer and fast-growing with more innovative ideas than others in the sector or industry. They tend to spend most of their financial resources on expansion and research and development (R&D) instead of paying out dividends to shareholders. Investors who mainly focus on future profits tend to prefer these stocks. Although most of the companies in this category tend to be newer and smaller, large and well-established companies (blue-chip stocks) like Google and Starbucks are defined as such.

Mutual Funds

Diversification

One of the long-debated arguments in securities investment is that individual stock investment is risky. It is especially true if you don't have enough money to adequately diversify your investment portfolio. If you invest all of your money in stocks of three companies and one of them goes out of business, for example, you'd lose one-third of your total investment. If you could invest in shares of hundreds or more of companies in many industries and several of them go bankrupt, the negative impact on your portfolio would be minimal. However, it costs a lot of money to buy individual company shares across the industries, and most investors don't have money to adequately diversify through individual stocks.

Mutual funds can address this dilemma of individual investors. Investment companies create mutual funds with pooled monies from many investors and invest in numerous stocks, bonds, commodities, and other funds. How many companies and how much any given mutual fund can invest in vary for different funds, and the detailed information can be found in the fund's prospectus, which can easily be found online. Unlike common stocks that represent direct ownership and give shareholders to vote on company matters, no direct voting rights are given to mutual fund investors on common stocks that they indirectly own. Fund managers (mutual fund company) can vote on behalf of their investors, but if dividends are paid on underlying stocks, investors receive the benefit.

Typically, names of mutual funds tell what any given fund's investment focus is. For example, a growth equity fund is invested in growth stocks, a bond fund invests in bonds, and an S&P 500 index fund invest in companies in the index, and so on. By investing in a well-diversified mutual fund, your money is said to be well-diversified, even if you only buy one share of the fund. Mutual funds are either actively or passively managed, and knowing the differences between the two is important.

Actively Managed Mutual Funds

Actively managed mutual funds, as the name says, are funds that are "actively" managed by fund managers. Fund managers buy and sell securities in their fund, as they deem necessary. The objective of actively managed funds is to perform better than the benchmark index. Because it costs money to have managers and other people who do extensive research on their fund's underlying securities, actively managed mutual funds typically cost more for investors to own. Actively managed funds are typically sold by financial advisors, and investors often pay between 0%- 6% in upfront fees, depending on the investment amount.

On top of the initial sales charge, actively managed mutual funds have an ongoing fund fee called an *expense ratio*, which includes costs for fund manager(s), advertisement, and administration. All mutual funds have an expense ratio, but actively managed funds tend to have higher rates than passively managed funds, typically between 0.8%-1.5.

There may be different classes such as A, B, C, D, I, R, etc., even for the same mutual fund. The main differences are the fees and the minimum amount required for an initial investment. One of the most wildly used actively managed mutual funds is class A shares. A shares have upfront fees, and they are typically sold by commission-based financial advisors. This upfront fee or commission is called *point* and ranges somewhere between 0%-6%, depending on the investment amounts. Smaller investment amounts are charged at a higher rate, while higher investment amounts are charged at a lower rate. For example, if your investment is less than $25,000, you may be charged at 6%, which is $1,500. If your investment is $200,000, then you may be charged at 3%, which is $6,000. Companies usually waive this upfront fee on an investment of $1 million or more. Other actively managed mutual fund classes may have no or low upfront charges but higher on-going fees. Pay attention to different classes and fees when you invest in funds. Read more information on mutual fund classes on FINRA.org (*Understanding Mutual Fund Classes*)

Passively Managed Mutual Funds (Index Funds)

Passively managed mutual funds, commonly known as index funds, are not actively managed by fund managers. In index funds, pooled monies are systematically invested in the securities as in the following benchmark index, such as the S&P 500, Total Stock Index, or NASDAQ Composite Index. Index funds don't need a big team of researchers/analysts because they mirror an index they follow, which considerably minimize management fees. Not all index funds have low costs, so you should check before investing. Index funds also may have different classes depending on the minimum investment amount: the ones with a higher minimum investment will have lower fees and vice versa. People who don't believe that fund managers can continuously outperform the market prefer index funds over actively managed funds. I invest the majority of my retirement savings in low-cost index funds, too.

ETFs (Exchange Traded Funds)

Hybrid between Stocks and Mutual Funds

ETFs are essentially mutual funds that are traded like stocks. Think of them as a hybrid of mutual funds and stocks. Like mutual funds, an ETF can invest in many types of securities such as stocks, bonds, options, etc. Like stocks, you can buy shares of an ETF anytime during a trading day, and the price can change as shares are bought and sold. Like mutual funds, they have an expense ratio, which is a combination of fees for fund management and administration.

Index ETFs generally have lower expense ratios and actively managed ETFs have higher fees, just like mutual funds. Like stocks, the minimum you can buy any given ETF is one share, as opposed to mutual funds that you can invest in a decimal number of a share. Like mutual funds, you don't directly own underlying securities in ETFs, and like stocks, transaction fees are charged on each ETF trading, unless waived by the brokerage company. There is a rising trend that companies are reducing transaction fees and other costs for competition, which is good for investors. Pay attention to fees when you trade ETFs.

What's Better: Mutual Funds or ETFs?

I generally prefer mutual funds as a long-term investment vehicle, but it depends on what investors want and need. If you like diversification that a mutual fund offers but want to trade with features that stocks offer such as a limit order and shorting, you can do ETFs. A *limit order* is when you set your price to buy/sell for a limited period, and when the price reaches your specified price, a transaction occurs. S*horting* is when investors borrow shares from a brokerage company to sell, betting that the price of the shares would go down in the future. By shorting, investors expect to profit by selling high with borrowed shares and buying (returning) shares back at a lower price.

Many mutual funds usually require a minimum amount of thousands of dollars. For example, you need a minimum of $3,000 to buy most Vanguard mutual funds. Some companies like Charles Schwab and Fidelity offer no or low required minimum amount on their mutual fund investment. If you don't have an initial amount for a mutual fund you like, you can start with an ETF that you can buy as little as one share. Be aware of transaction costs, if any, as they will lower your potential earnings. Once you have saved enough for the mutual fund you like, you can exchange the ETFs for the mutual fund. Not considering trading fees, ETFs' stock-like trading features can be beneficial for savvy investors.

There may be a specific industry in which you want to invest, but only ETFs may provide such exposure. For example, my husband recently wanted to invest in new technology that he couldn't find a mutual fund for, so he bought ETFs, instead.

Motifs

ETFs with Investment Selection Control

Mutual funds could address the risks of individual stock investing. And ETFs could address the inflexibility of mutual fund investing by allowing investors to trade ETFs like individual stocks. Neither mutual funds nor ETFs allow investors to choose what underlying securities to invest inside of the fund. Now, motifs provide investors ultimate control. If a given ETF has 30 underlying securities, for instance, you cannot change the number or the proportion of the securities inside of the ETF. With motifs, you can select a pre-built motif and delete underlying securities, add new ones, control the weight of each underlying security, essentially creating and managing your own fund. Suppose you like energy-related funds but don't want your money invested in companies that are not environment friendly. Then you can create a new motif with stocks you want or take an existing one and modify it as you like, which you cannot do in a mutual fund or an ETF. Unlike mutual funds and ETFs, you own underlying stocks with voting rights, and there's no fund management fee because you are acting as a fund manager in your motif. If other investors trade the motifs you created, you can get paid.

Other Securities

Options

Options are contracts that you trade a "right" to buy or sell underlying securities. For example, let's say you own 100 shares of ABC stocks and believe ABC will do well in the future, but you want to protect your investment just in case you're wrong. Then you can buy an option contract (one option contract has 100 shares of underlying securities) that grants a right for you to sell your ABC stocks at a certain price (strike) in case the price goes down. On the other side of the option contract is someone who sells the contract, obligating himself to buy ABC shares at a certain price if you choose to sell them. He sells such contract because he doesn't think the ABC shares will go down before the option contract expires. If the stock price does go down at the end of the option contract term, you can exercise your "right" to sell the stocks at an agreed-upon price. The person who sold the option contract to you must buy the stocks at the set (higher than the market) price per the contract. If your stock prices end up going up higher than the contract price, you won't want to sell them at a lower price, of course. In that case, you can let go of your contractual "right" to sell the stocks. What you lose is the price you paid for the option contract that gave you the right to sell. The person who sold the contract profits in this case.

Futures

Future contracts mostly work the same way as options, except that people who are involved have a legal obligation to fulfill the contract. If the above option example were a future contract, you would have to sell the stocks, regardless of price at the end of the contract term. Future contracts are commonly used by investors/companies that want to protect themselves from the fluctuation of price in the future, whether it is a price of goods or foreign exchange rates. For example, say an orange juice company wants to keep the production cots constant. If there is an orange shortage and the price skyrockets, the company won't be able to produce its products at the current price. The juice company wants to have an arrangement with orange farmers to deliver a certain amount of oranges at a certain price when they harvest. The company will benefit if there is an orange shortage in the coming harvest season, but if there's a surplus of oranges, the farmers will benefit because they can sell their produce at a higher agreed-upon price.

Hedge Funds

Hedge funds are like mutual funds, but with fewer regulations and targeted for accreted investors who are institutions or wealthy individuals. Hedge funds can be invested in any type of securities and can use leverage, meaning the funds can take out a loan. The goal of hedge funds is to make as much money as possible in a relatively short period usually within several years. Fees are high with an average fund management fee of 2% *plus* about 20% of profits. By nature, hedge funds tend to be more aggressive and, therefore, risky by definition.

Private Equity Funds

Private equity funds purchase financially distressed companies, restructure to increase the value, and sell them for profits. They typically target already established companies that are in financial distress for various reasons. Private equity funds usually take over companies they invest so that they can have total control in restructuring. They restructure management, lay off employees, sell assets, get more loans, or whatever actions the fund managers deem necessary to increase the value of the company to sell. They generally work on one company at a time before moving on.

Venture Capital Funds

Venture capital funds work similarly as private equity funds, but they typically invest in new startup companies and don't take total control over management. Unlike private equity funds that invest in established companies regardless of industry, venture capital funds mostly invest in start-up companies with high potential, usually with new technology. They invest in many companies simultaneously in general, unlike private equity funds that typically work on one company at a time.

Indexes and Index Funds

An index is nothing more than a measurement that tracks ups and downs of certain things. Think of CPI (Consumer Price Index) that is a measurement of inflation, telling us if the prices of goods and services that we frequently use went up or down in a given past period. There are many indexes that measure different things in the economy. As for tracking movements of stock markets, there are three major indexes: DOW Jones, S&P 500, and NASDAQ Composite Index.

Dow Jones

One of the oldest securities market indexes, The Dow Jones Industrial Average tracks stock prices of 30 large US companies. It was created by Charles Dow, who was a co-founder of Dow Jones Industry and editor of The Wall Street Journal. When created in 1896, it only had 12 companies, but eventually increased to 30. The list of the companies in the index changes over time, with Apple and Nike being two of the most recent addition. The editors at *The Wall Street Journal* decide what companies are included.

S&P 500

Started in 1957, the Standard & Poor (S&P) 500 Composite Stock Price Index tracks ups and downs of 500 US large company stock prices. The index committee, owned by McGraw Hill Financial, decides rules on which companies are included or excluded on the list. The index is affected proportionally by the weight of the 500 companies' market capitalization.

NASDAQ Composite Index

Originated in 1971, NASDAQ Composite Index is calculated based on stocks traded in the NASDAQ Stock Exchange, which has over 3,000 companies. Unlike S&P 500 and Dow Jones, it includes stocks of international companies that are registered and traded in the exchange.

Index Funds

People cannot directly invest in an index, as it is just a measurement and not securities that can be bought and sold. Instead, they can invest in index mutual funds or ETFs that are created by investment companies. As explained earlier, index mutual funds and index ETFs invest pooled monies in securities based on the index composite that they follow, rearranging allocations according to changes made by the index composite. Index funds from different companies usually deliver different returns, even if they all track the same index. That is because of several factors, such as rebalancing frequency and fees. See an article discussing this topic on Morningstar.com (*Same Index, Different Returns*)

Investment Costs

Why Fees Matter

For most people who don't have enough money to diversify with individual stocks, mutual funds can be a great investment choice because they can adequately diversify small amounts. One of the problems with mutual fund investment is complexity associated with fees. In other words, it is not easy for most people to understand how much they actually pay in fees in any given year. (Do you think that is coincident?) Depending on funds, the type of account and the investment company, there may be many fees in different names. When all these fees add up, they can greatly reduce your asset accumulation over time. For example, 1% extra annual fees can reduce your total assets by more than 30% over 30 years. While fees should not be the only factor in an investment decision, ignoring them would be a big mistake. Warren Buffet, one of the world's greatest investors, warns how fees can hurt investors and highly recommends low-cost index funds (Forbes.com - *Warren Buffet's Single-Best Piece of Advice*). Visit SEC.org for more information on how fees can affect your money (*How Fees and Expenses Affect Your Investment Portfolio*).

I want to reiterate about retirement plan fees here, as most people's retirement assets are in a company plan like 401(k) and 403(b). As I mentioned in the Retirement chapter, sponsors of qualified retirement plans (your company) have a responsibility to do their due diligence to provide a plan with reasonable fees. Understand that retirement plan fees are often based on the size of assets: the more assets your plan has in total, the lower % you may pay in general. According to MarketWatch.com, 401(k) plans with large companies pay about 0.5%, medium-sized companies 0.85%, and small companies 1.4% on average (*9 things you need to know about 401(k) fees*) That is on top of an annual administration fee that you, a plan participant, may pay, usually $30-$35/yr. If you are saving a small amount per month from your paycheck and if your employer doesn't provide any match, it may make more sense for you to invest that money in an IRA with lower fees. Let's say that you want to save $100 a month from your paycheck into your 401(k) account, and your company doesn't offer any match. Further assume that the average investment fee is 1% and the annual administration fee is $35. Then you'll pay $47 in one year, which is almost 4% of your $1,200 annual savings! Without an employer match, it would be difficult for your nest egg to grow much after paying such fees. If your diversified 401(k) assets don't seem to grow much even in the "good" market, fees are likely to blame. Don't hesitate to bring it to the person in charge of the plan, as this can benefit everybody, including the participating owner(s).

How to Start Securities Investment

It Is About What You Invest and Fees

Where you open your investment accounts doesn't necessarily matter, when it comes to "safety" of your assets, as investments are not generally protected from potential loss. If, for example, you own shares of Apple

Inc., whether you have your account at Wells Fargo or Fidelity doesn't affect your investment. The assets inside of your account are separate from the assets of the company that is holding your account. As long as Apple's doing well, you'll profit, though you'll lose money if not. What matters is what you invest inside of your account and how much total fees you pay. Account maintenance fees and trading fees are something you should pay attention to and avoid if possible.

Full-Service Advisors

If you need an adviser to hold your hand in every step of your investment, you may want a financial adviser near you. Of course, such service costs money. You would pay either commission through actively managed mutual funds or a percentage of your investment assets or both, depending on the type of a financial adviser (company) you hire and securities you invest. Generally, financial advisers with well-known companies require a minimum amount to invest with them. That doesn't necessarily mean more profits for you or higher qualifications of the advisers. See the next chapter, Financial Advisers, to learn more about different types of financial advisers.

Hourly Rate Service for Initial Help

If you need a local adviser but want to minimize fees, local fee-only financial advisers with a flat or hourly rate may work for you. They can help you with overall financial planning and set up an automatic investment. It can initially cost you some hundreds to thousands of dollars but can potentially save you a great deal of money over time because there are no ongoing fees. You need to monitor and modify your financial plans as situations change, so I recommend you see the planner once a year or if you have a life event that can affect your finance, whichever comes first. If you are over 10 years away from retirement and have no change that can affect your finances, you can see an advisor every other year, in my opinion. It may be the most cost-effective way to get personalized and in-person professional service, though actual money savings may vary by individuals. Most financial planners who provide hourly services are independent, often working for themselves, as large financial companies don't usually allow their advisers to provide such services.

Robo-Advisors

If you feel comfortable using the Internet to manage your accounts but need some help with investment decisions, you can consider a robo-advisor. When you open an account with a robo-advisor online, you'll be asked a series of questions before recommendations are provided. They charge ongoing investment management fees that are typically lower than full-service local advisers'. However, because you pay continuing fees based on your investment assets, your costs may be higher than when working with a local adviser with hourly service, depending on your investment assets. Betterment, Wealthfront, and Charles Schwab are some of the leading robo-advisors.

Mutual Fund Companies

If you just want to follow the advice of Warren Buffet, you can open an account with a mutual fund company and buy low-cost index funds. If you want to invest in S&P 500 index funds from Vanguard, for example, open an account on Vanguard.com and buy Vanguard index funds without paying any transaction fees or service fee to an adviser. If you have a sizable investment asset, consider funds with higher minimum amounts such as $10,000, $25,000 or $50,000, as they tend to have lower expense ratios. This is the least expensive way when it comes to diversified investment for most people, but it could be overwhelming. The more serious potential problem that can arise when you do it by yourself is that you may not be able to see a bigger picture: investment is one piece of financial planning, as there are many other parts such as insurance, education planning, tax planning, estate planning, etc.

What If You Feel You Can See Future Google?

There's no "beating the market" or searching for a "hidden gem" in an index fund investment. You may argue about why you should invest in 'boring' index funds when you feel like you can see future rock stars, like Google or Apple in their infancy. I hear this argument from many people who are working in a professional field. Since they work in a specific industry that they know well, many tend to believe that they can pick the future gem in their field. I recently had this conversation with someone who is in IT and wanted to invest in disruptive technology, a word describing a new technology that is expected to put a current industry out of business. Cars, for example, quickly put horse farms and wagon makers out of business. Electric vehicles and natural energy from solar panels and windmills are expected to dominate the future, forcing traditional energy providers such as the oil and coal industry out of business.

We all agree that technology will continue to innovate and be an integral part of our future economy, but we don't know how long it will be before any new technology takes off. We know some companies at the center of innovation will become successful, but we don't know which ones will dominate the industry in the future. We can easily see which companies are currently leading in any given technology, but there's no guarantee that they will continue to lead. Even if we do choose the future leaders, what if the investment takes longer to capitalize than we expected? There are too many variables that we cannot foresee, and more importantly, most of us cannot afford to be wrong or partially right. Statistically speaking, the chance of losing money from investing in hundreds of well-established companies is considerably lower than the chance of anyone picking some "future gem" today. In other words, it is highly risky to heavily invest in a handful of companies, regardless of the industry. I'm not saying you shouldn't invest in companies that you believe in. Instead, I'm saying you should invest the amount that won't hurt you too much, just in case you're wrong or too early to realize the boom. After some research and calculations together, the person I mentioned earlier decided to invest about 5-7% of his money in one stock and a few ETFs for that technology, and the rest in low-cost index funds.

Chapter 8
FINANCIAL ADVISERS

Unlike for CPAs and attorneys, the industry for financial advisers is not standardized, and people can call themselves by many similar titles. It is crucial for investors to distinguish qualified planners and understand how advisers are paid so they can determine what they pay is worth the service they receive.

1. The Reality
2. Suitability vs. Fiduciary
3. How Financial Advisers Are Paid
4. Who to Hire

The Reality

Industry

Companies exist to make money. They won't spend their time in providing products and services to people or community if there's little potential to profit. That is why most investment companies don't open a branch in low-income neighborhoods, and many financial advisers don't even bother to talk to individuals who don't have a large sum of money to invest or make a certain level of income. As a result, people with modest income that could greatly benefit from good financial advice have been underserved for too long. Thanks to technology, there is an increasing number of small investors who become savvy and know how to take advantage of what used to be available only to the wealthy. Also increasing is a new type of financial advisers who are willing to work with people regardless of their income or investment assets.

Many Titles, No Standardization

Do you know the differences between a financial advisor (with -OR), financial adviser (with -ER), financial planner, financial consultant, wealth manager, wealth advisor, investment adviser, etc.? If no, you're not alone. I don't either. Further confusion **arises** when people with the same title have a different focus area, and those who do the same work can have different titles. Some people refer to financial planners as those with a highly regarded CFP® certification, although that doesn't stop anyone whose focus is selling financial products for commission calling him/ herself by that title. I've seen insurance agents and mortgage lenders calling themselves by one of the titles. That is why I use different words such as financial adviser (with -ER), financial advisor (with -OR), and financial planner throughout the book, too. There's no one correct title.

The reason for this confusion is because those titles are not standardized. To become a CPA or a lawyer, for instance, you must obtain the required education and experience and pass standard exams. There are no current standardized education or exams that individuals must undertake before calling themselves a financial adviser or a similar title. That is why SEC.gov tells the public that it "does not endorse any financial professional titles," saying those titles are generally "marketing tools." It further warns, "not to rely solely on a title to determine whether a financial professional has the expertise that you need" (*Making Sense of Financial Professional Titles*). Be sure to visit the website with invaluable information in simple English. It will clear up much confusion and may help you avoid costly mistakes.

Investment Advisers and Registration

Regardless of a job title, however, people who advise on securities investment in the US (and get paid for it) must pass standardized securities exams (Series 7, Series 66, etc.) and be registered. The passing of a few securities exams and registration are not a guarantee of anyone's qualifications, needless to say. No college degree or experience in the finance field is required to sit for many securities exams, and people with a few months of study can usually pass the exams to be allowed to advise on securities.

SEC vs. State Registration and Brokers vs. IARs

Depending on the number of state registrations and asset under management (AUM), companies (and advisers) can be registered with the Securities and Exchange Commission (SEC) or a state(s). Large companies (and their advisors) are registered with the SEC, and small firms (and their advisors) are usually registered with the state(s). Individuals who work for a broker-dealer firm are called broker-dealer representatives, although they are commonly called brokers. I'll call them brokers here for simplicity. People who work for a registered investment adviser (RIA) are registered as investment adviser representatives (IAR) that are commonly called investment advisers.

Checking Registration and Background

Investors can check brokers and investment advisers' registration, any known disciplinary actions, and personal backgrounds such as education and experience. For brokers, visit *Broker Check* on BrokerCheck.FINRA.org, and for investment advisers, visit SEC.gov (*Investment Adviser Public Disclosure*). You can also get the same information by contacting your state regulators on NASAA.org (*Contact Your Regulator*). North American Securities Administrators Association (NASAA) is an organization of state securities regulators whose main goal is to protect investors from fraud. If you are not sure how any adviser whom you want to hire is registered, check both sites. In my case, I used to be registered as a broker while working for a large broker-dealer, but after starting my own registered investment adviser (RIA) firm, I am now registered as an investment adviser representative (IAR). If someone wants to check my registration and background, she will have to use both sites, though the information largely overlaps.

Suitability vs. Fiduciary

Understanding the difference between the suitability and fiduciary standards can save you a headache in distinguishing who you may want to work with. Brokers follow a suitability standard, which requires them to provide 'suitable' recommendations to investors, given limited options. The advice or recommended products may or may not be for the *best interest* of their clients. As long as they are 'suitable' or 'reasonable' for investors, that is allowed. That is not to say that there aren't any brokers who do what's best for their clients, rather, they are not legally obligated to put their clients' best interest above their own.

A fiduciary, on the other hand, has a stricter standard that obligates financial advisers to work for the best interest of their clients. In a simple example, let's say two financial products are almost identical to each other, and one has higher fees than the other. The one with lower fees would be more beneficial for the client in this case, though the one with higher fees will benefit the adviser who receives commission from the sales. As long as the product with higher fees is 'reasonable' and 'suitable', the adviser following the suitability standard is likely to recommend the one that will earn his company (and him) higher commission. The advisor with a fiduciary standard is obligated to recommend the one for the client's best interest, which is the one with lower fees. All investment advisers are to follow fiduciary standards. For more information on differences between suitability and fiduciary, see an article on Forbes.com (*The Difference Between Fiduciary and Suitability Standards*).

More financial advisors in the industry follow the suitability standard than fiduciary, and it has allowed many of them to sell products that are more beneficial to their own pocket than their clients'. There naturally has been the public outcry to protect investors from those advisors who practice for self-interest. The Department of Labor (DOL)'s Conflict of Interest Rule, commonly known as Fiduciary Rule, was expected to become effective in mid-2017 after a few delays, but as late 2018, it is still uncertain if it'll ever be enacted. Even if the rule was enforced in 2017, it was going to apply to retirement accounts only. I'll leave it up to your wild imagination why this was limited only to retirement accounts and why even that is so hard to implement. If you want to learn more about it, read an article on Investopedia.com (*The DOL Fiduciary Rule Explained*)

Demand Fiduciary from Your Advisor

Even if this fiduciary rule were in effect today, the policy itself wouldn't protect investors well from unethical financial advisers, including IARs who are supposed to act as a fiduciary at all times. Ken Fisher, a founder of Fisher Investments and an author of many books, strongly suggests investors demand their adviser to sign a pledge to act under the fiduciary standard strictly. He says that the letter should contain clear wording of defining fiduciary duty. Mr. Fisher recommends walking away if an adviser refuses to sign such form. Read his insightful article and an example of a fiduciary letter on USAToday.com (*Don't Roll Over for This 401k and IRA Ripoff*).

Chapter 8 | FINANCIAL ADVISERS

How Financial Advisers Are Paid

Working with a financial adviser who is a fiduciary is indeed important. The reality is that most financial advisers, fiduciary or not, are under constant pressure by their boss to bring in more revenue. Think about it. Companies are there to make money, and the managers' utmost duty is to maximize the company's (shareholders') profits. The managers' job security (and advisers', too) and their income often depend on how much money advisers bring in. This reality explains the high turnover rate among new financial advisers. It also leads investors to rightfully question how honestly their adviser can work in the best interest of clients above his/her own. The best way for investors to protect themselves, in my opinion, is by understanding how advisers are paid (how investors pay), eliminate circumstances for potential conflict of interest, and evaluate if their service is worth the fees. There are three major ways that financial advisers get paid: commission-based, fee-only, and fee-based.

Commission-based

Commission-based advisers make money by selling actively managed mutual funds and insurance products. Commission rates vary by different financial products and investment amounts. They also make money from trading securities, and the more frequent trading activities, the more commissions they get. This unethical practice of excessive trading called churning is one of the reasons many people criticize the commission-based compensation method. Since commission-based advisers make money by selling products and from trading securities, investors don't pay their advisors directly for their service, which leads some people to incorrectly think that they get "free advice." If your commission-based advisor recommends you to invest $50,000 in a financial product that pays 5% commission, you will end up paying $2,500. The advice is not that "free," is it?

Fee-only

Financial advisers who are fee-only do not get commissions, meaning they don't sell financial products. Instead, they charge ongoing service fees directly from their clients usually based on their investment assets. They recommend financial products such as insurance, as deemed necessary, but they don't get any compensation from companies whose products they recommend. Their service fees usually range between 0.5-1.5%, depending on the investment assets or a flat amount like $5,000 per year. Because of transparency on fees with no commission or incentives from products or trading, fee-only advisers are wildly favored by consumer advocates over commission-based advisers.

One problem with the fee-only structure is that as long as the fees are based on the amount of investment assets, advisers are limited to favor the rich. Think about it. One percent of $1 million is $10,000, while the same 1% on $100,000 is $1,000. Assuming the time to provide service is similar for both clients, who would you rather work with? Of course, you would prefer to work with the rich client because you can make more money for your time. That is why many fee-only financial advisers require minimum investment assets such as $250,000 or $500,000. They may accept young professionals as clients, even though they may not have accumulated the minimum required investment asset, but they often require minimum flat fees such as $3,000 or $5,000 per year.

People who don't want to work with a commission-based financial advisor but cannot afford a fee-only adviser are left underserved in this system. This niche market created hourly service and a flat fee per service. Fee-only advisers who have flexibility in fee adjustments, usually because they are independent, often provide these services along with a percentage fee based on investment assets. Their hourly rates vary somewhere between $150-$400, and they also offer on-going service on a monthly flat fee.

Fee-based

This is a hybrid structure invented by commission-based firms that felt threatened by the rising popularity of fee-only advisers. (Do you think it is a coincidence that so many people are confused between fee-only and. fee-based?). They get a combination of fees and commission. They are paid from clients through a percentage of clients' investment and sell other financial products for a commission. For that reason, a potential conflict of interest exists in this type of pay structure. See article on USNews.com (*A Guide to Financial Advisor Fee Structure*) and ChicagoTribune.com (*Fee-Only Financial Advisers are Different from Fee-Based*).

Who to Hire

Working with fee-only advisers who are fiduciaries is indeed highly recommended. They are legally obligated to put their clients' interest above all, and their transparent fees allow investors to analyze if the service received is worth the costs. But I should point out that even fee-only advisers *could* have room for a conflict of interest in their advice as well, especially if they are under pressure by their boss, as most advisers are. The more assets fee-only advisers have under their management, the more money they (and their company) make. If you have a $500,000 investment asset in a non-retirement account with relatively low returns and have a high interest rate loan of $200,000, for example, it would make more financial sense to pull some of your investment and pay the loan. However, if your fee-only adviser is under pressure to find more clients (bring in more money), it would be difficult for him/her to advise you to pay off the loan from the investments. That's why knowing exactly how much you pay and determining if the service you receive is worth the costs is most important, in my opinion. With a fee-only advisor, it should be easy for you to calculate how much you pay, whether it's a percentage of your investment or a flat rate.

If you have a commission-based or fee-based advisor, it may be difficult for you to figure out exactly how much you pay because most fees are paid indirectly, and your statement won't show it. If necessary, don't hesitate to ask the adviser to write down in a dollar amount how much you pay both directly and indirectly and evaluate if his/her service is worth the money you pay.

If you don't have enough investable assets or high income to hire a fee-only adviser, or if you don't want to pay 1% or whatever amount that is charged by a typical fee-only adviser, find a fee-only adviser who also provides an hourly or monthly flat rate. I like this simplest fee structure because it eliminates any potential for unbiased advice. For me, as one who provides hourly and flat fee service, how much one has or makes doesn't affect my advice in any way. Those who need my monthly service are usually small business owners who need help in administering their retirement plan. As for my clients, since they directly pay me, they can easily evaluate if the service received is worth the costs.

While using hourly pay-on-demand service may be the cheapest and the most unbiased option for many investors, I must point out that using this type of service can have people too focused on fees and not pay attention to the bigger and more important picture. As I explain throughout the book, financial planning is much more than investment, and ignoring what a qualified adviser can do to help you with overall financial stability can be a very costly and irreversible mistake. I've seen many people who are not financially savvy yet too focused on saving and didn't hire anyone, which resulted in financial instability at the end. I much rather you pay higher on-going fees for a qualified adviser than not using anyone, jeopardizing your financial stability.

Education and Qualifications of Advisers

I do believe that most advisers want to and try to do what's best for their clients. The problem is that they won't know what's best if they don't have adequate knowledge in overall personal finance. For example, if all one adviser knows is insurance products and actively managed mutual funds, he would give advice based on the products he knows, which may not be for the best interest of his clients. That's why finding an adviser who's well qualified is critical to effectively achieve financial stability.

One of the highly recommended certifications for financial advisers is Certified Financial Planner (CFP®). To become a CFP® professional, one must take classes that cover personal finance matters such as investment, retirement planning, insurance, personal income taxes, and estate planning and pass a two-day exam. They also need three years of experience or equivalent and a bachelor's degree, as well as extensive ethics education. See more information on CFP® qualifications on CFP.net (*CFP® Certification Requirements*). All CFP® professionals are supposed to act in the best interest of their clients, but they may be limited to follow suitability standards in reality, depending on what employer they work for. That is why it is essential, as Mr. Fisher recommends, to have your adviser sign a fiduciary agreement. Other certifications that are also recommended are CFA (Chartered Financial Analyst) and PFS (Personal Financial Specialist), according to Investopedia.com (*The Top 3 Financial Advisor Credentials*).

Where to Find Them

NAPFA (The National Association of Personal Financial Advisor) is one of the recommended websites that you can use to search for fee-only CFP® professionals (or those who are in the process of getting it) who also pledge to always work as a fiduciary. They are strictly prohibited from receiving or paying any compensation from or to a third party that can hinder them from acting as a fiduciary planner. Not all fee-only CFP® professionals who are fiduciary are registered in the websites, as I am one of those who could join but decided not to (I'm frugal). Interview several advisers and don't hesitate to ask questions before hiring one: it is your money. Once you find one you like, please listen to your adviser, as your financial success depends on good advice and your follow-through actions.

It Is About Teamwork, Too.

Another important thing you should understand is that there are many areas involved in personal financial planning such as, but not limited to, Social Security, insurance, investment, retirement planning, estate planning, education planning, taxes, credit and debt management, loans, etc. All of these areas can further have subcategories with specialized professionals. Although a highly qualified financial planner should have a good understanding of all or most areas that affect his clients' finances, the reality is that no one person can have as much knowledge as professionals in all fields. For instance, I have studied personal taxes and even write a chapter about it, but I don't have in-depth knowledge in taxation as tax professionals do. Likewise, many CPAs understand retirement plans, but they usually don't know the details and lack overall financial planning skills. That is why I work closely with my clients' tax advisors and don't hesitate to bring in other professionals if necessary. Financial planners, in my view, are like primary doctors in the medical field who work with other specialists to keep their patients healthy. If you see a financial professional who claims to know everything in personal finance without supporting education, be careful. That is not too different from a primary doctor claiming to know, without supporting education, how to personally fix all health problems in your eyes, teeth, heart, skin, bones, etc.

Chapter 9
PERSONAL BANKRUPTCY

Personal bankruptcy provides a fresh start to those who cannot repay debts. It is vital for people to realize that anybody can quickly fall into financial ruin by losing a job or being sick. Thus, understanding what's available should be a part of one's financial planning.

1. Chapter 13 Bankruptcy
2. Chapter 7 Bankruptcy
3. Top Reasons for Personal Bankruptcy

As US Courts states, "Bankruptcy helps people who can no longer pay their debts get a fresh start by liquidating assets to pay their debts or by creating a repayment plan" (USCourts.gov). There are two types of bankruptcy that individuals can file: Chapter 13 and Chapter 7 bankruptcy.

Chapter 13 Bankruptcy

Chapter 13 is a "milder" type of bankruptcy because you get to keep your properties, unlike Chapter 7 bankruptcy where your properties are liquidated to pay creditors. In Chapter 13 bankruptcy, you make payments that are reorganized by the court for a limited period, and the remaining dischargeable debt is canceled. Individuals who have less than $394,725 in unsecured debt and $1,184,200 in secured debt can file this type of bankruptcy (2018). Unsecured debt includes, but not limited to, credit card debt, medical debt, rents, etc., and secured debt includes mortgage, car loan, and any debt that has collateral.

To be eligible to file Chapter 13 bankruptcy, you must have income and be current on your income tax filing status for the past recent four years. In other words, if you don't have income or didn't file your taxes, you can't file for Chapter 13 bankruptcy. Bankruptcy is a federal law, but eligibilities and exemptions may vary depending on the state you live and the judge who rules your case. Visit USCourts.gov for more information on Chapter 13 eligibility (*Chapter 13 - Bankruptcy Basics*).

Your debt is discharged after the agreed payments are made, which takes about 3-5 years. Most consumer debt such as credit card debt, car loan, and medical debt are dischargeable unless a creditor(s) successfully objects that you committed fraud with no intention to pay back. Mortgages usually are excluded in the bankruptcy process, and even if they are included, the original term (15 or 30 years, for example) is usually kept. If there is a second mortgage and the current home price is less than the total mortgage debt, it may be categorized as an unsecured loan and allowed to be discharged.

Some debts are not dischargeable through bankruptcy. Most student loans, income taxes owed, child support and alimony, judgment from personal injury, and criminal penalty are some examples that are not discharged. Debts that are not listed in a bankruptcy filing and intentional fraudulent debts will survive, too. For more information on which debts can survive the bankruptcy, see Nolo.com, a reputable website that connects people with lawyers (*Debts That Survive Chapter 13 Bankruptcy*).

For one to use this legal process to be allowed to have a "fresh start," it is imperative that he follows all the rules until the bankruptcy case is closed. Be present for your court dates and make payments on time. Understand all your obligations and follow through; otherwise, the bankruptcy case can be canceled, or the judge can order it to convert to Chapter 7 bankruptcy. If it is canceled, you must wait six months before you can restart the process.

Chapter 7 Bankruptcy

In Chapter 7 bankruptcy, you surrender your properties that can be liquidated to pay creditors, and the remaining debt is discharged. The required eligibility is stricter for Chapter 7 than Chapter 13, and you must earn less than the median income of the state for your family size. If your discretionary income (after essential living costs including, but not limited to, housing, utility, medical expenses, transportation costs, food, etc.) is more than $12,850 in the past 60 months, you won't be eligible. If you paid more than 25% (or $77,000) of your unsecured debt during the period, you won't be allowed to file Chapter 7 bankruptcy, unless you successfully argue to be allowed to file based on your unique circumstances. You can find your state's median income for your family size by searching online. If your income is above your state's median income, you need to pass the means test. Check out LegalConsumer.com for means test calculator (*Means Test Calculator*).

As in Chapter 13 bankruptcy, some debts such as most student loans, taxes, child support and alimony, judgment against personal injury are not discharged in Chapter 7, either. See more information on nondischargeable debts on Nolo.com (*Nondischargeable Debts in Chapter 7 Bankruptcy*). Also, for differences between Chapter 13 and Chapter 7 bankruptcy, visit FindLaw.com (*Chapter 7 vs. Chapter 13 Bankruptcy*)

The bankruptcy laws are there to help individuals and companies to have a fresh start. They provide exemptions for home, car, and others, but the amount may vary depending on your state and your situation. Because you need first to pass the means test and there are exemptions, the majority of people who file Chapter 7 bankruptcy get to keep most of their properties. For information on Chapter 7 exemptions, see *Exemptions in Chapter 7 Bankruptcy* and for dollar amounts of federal exemptions, see *The Federal Bankruptcy Exemptions* (both on Nolo.com).

Notice that retirement assets are protected from general creditors even in bankruptcy. IRAs are protected at about $1.3 million, though your state may have different limits, but most employer plans such as a pension plan, 401(k), 403(b), SIMPLE IRA, 457(b), and SEP IRA are protected with no limit. You can literally have millions of dollars in your 401(k) and keep 'em all even after several bankruptcies. I hope you fully understand how a good financial plan can protect your assets even from an unfortunate event like bankruptcy and why you should try to maximize your retirement contributions each year, if at all possible. Some parties that your retirement assets are vulnerable to are family members for child support and alimony and the government for unpaid taxes and federal student loans.

Top Reasons for Personal Bankruptcy

People file for bankruptcy for many reasons, and although orders may differ depending on what data you see, the following five seem most common: medical expenses, job loss, credit card debt, divorce/separation, unexpected expenses.

As discussed in the Health Insurance section, too many Americans cannot afford good health insurance with low out-of-pocket costs. Health insurance premiums for American workers have gone up by 83% from 2005 to 2015. The deductibles went up 255% from 2006 to 2015, according to NPR.org (*Medical Bills Still Take A Big Toll, Even With Insurance*). The article reports that 26% of Americans said that health care related expenses caused them a severe financial problem, which should surprise no one that medical costs are the top reason for personal bankruptcy in the US. Unless you are rich with millions to spare for health care costs, we all are just one sickness away from financial ruin in America.

When you look at other reasons for bankruptcy, they are closely related; losing a job or getting divorced will also put enormous stress on one's finances. Studies show that an increasing number of people are relying on credit cards to pay for essential living expenses such as food and gas. If you are in financial distress now, you are not alone. Please don't wait until you're forced for bankruptcy and seek help as soon as possible. Proactive planning will reduce your stress and give you more options to protect what you have. Even if you are financially comfortable today, there's no guarantee that you'll continue to have that level of income or be healthy to work until retirement. For all of us who have to work for a living, bankruptcy is closer than you may think. Planning for the worst will get you farther away from financial ruin.

Chapter 10
PERSONAL TAXES

There are different taxes that individuals pay throughout their life. Reducing tax liabilities is essential to save more to achieve financial stability, and it starts with understanding what taxes you pay.

1. Payroll Tax
2. Federal & State Income Tax
3. Long-term Capital Gains Tax
4. AMT (Alternative Minimum Tax)
5. Sales Tax
6. Property Tax
7. Estate/Gift Tax
8. Tax Problems?

Chapter 10 | PERSONAL TAXES

The purpose of this chapter is to help you understand how many different ways that you pay taxes, so you can plan to minimize them, if possible. Too many people believe that financial stability is achieved by making more money at work and through high investment returns. While more income and higher investment return certainly will help, most people have limited opportunities and abilities to make a fortune during their lifetime. Therefore, reducing spending, which can increase savings, becomes an integral key to financial stability for most people. Taxes are a large part of "spending" that takes a big bite out of our limited income, as you should already know. I discuss a small number of taxes that are most relevant to individuals, and I do not go into deductions in detail. This chapter is intended for general education only and not for your tax calculation purposes. For information or your specific tax issues, consult a tax professional.

Payroll Tax

Earned Income

There are different types of income such as earned income that is from working, capital gains that are from investment, retirement income that you withdraw from your pre-tax retirement accounts, rental income, alimony, insurance payout, inheritance, gift, etc., and they may be subject to different tax rules. Payroll taxes are imposed on earned income, which is money you make from working, whether you're working for someone or yourself. Wages, tips, and self-employment income are examples of earned income. See IRS.gov for what's included in earned income (*What is Earned Income?*). Payroll taxes, also known as FICA (Federal Insurance Contributions Act) have two parts: Social Security tax and Medicare tax.

Social Security Tax

Social Security tax is currently at 6.2%, but taxable income is capped at $128,400 ($132,900 in 2019). That means the maximum Social Security tax that anyone pays in 2018 is $7,961, whether you make $128,400 or $1 million ($8,240 in 2019). Your employer also pays the same amount in Social Security tax, so the total of 12.4% between you and your employer is paid into Social Security. If you are self-employed, you pay a total of 12.4%, but 50% of it is deducted when filing taxes each year. Your Social Security benefit after retirement is calculated based on your reported earned income (in other words, how much you paid into the system).

Medicare Tax

Medicare tax is 1.45%, and there's no income cap. Both employees and employers pay 1.45% each, with a total of 2.9%. There's an extra 0.9% Medicare tax on income over $200,000 ($250,000 for joint filers) per year. Employers don't match this extra tax.

Through payroll taxes, employees who make $128,400 ($132,900 in 2019) or less per year pay a total of 7.65% of their total earned income for Social Security and Medicare taxes. Social Security and Medicare are two of the largest spending programs at about 40% of the total federal budget. See more information on payroll taxes on IRS.gov (*Social Security and Medicare Withholding Rates*).

Federal & State Income Tax

Federal and state income taxes are applied to ordinary income which includes, but not limited to, earned income, retirement income from non-Roth accounts, rental income, interest income, gambling and lottery winning and other awards, short-term (1 year or less) investment profits etc. It is important to differentiate ordinary incomes from earned income because ordinary income is *not* subject to payroll taxes. All earned income is subject to payroll taxes *and* ordinary income taxes. For example, if you made $10,000 from working, then the total amount will be subject to 7.65% payroll taxes *and* ordinary income taxes. But if you made the same amount from renting a property, which is ordinary income, then you will just pay income taxes, but not payroll taxes. Ordinary income taxes have two parts: federal income tax and state income tax.

Federal Income Tax

Federal income tax currently has seven brackets ranging between 10% and 37%, depending on income and tax filing status. In the following table, MFJ is married couples filing income tax jointly, and HH is head of household.

Rate	Singles, Income over	MFJ, Income over	HH, Income over
10%	$0	$0	$0
12%	$9,525	$19,050	$13,600
22%	$38,700	$77,400	$51,800

24%	$82,500	$165,000	$82,500
32%	$157,500	$315,000	$157,500
35%	$200,000	$400,000	$200,000
37%	$500,000	$600,000	$500,000

These are new tax brackets effective 2018. When comparing to the previous rules, the highest rate has come down to 37% from 39.6%, and income limit for each rate has increased, resulting in a decrease in overall tax liabilities for most taxpayers. One thing that I want to point out is that these tax rates apply gradually. For example, if you and your spouse together make $200,000 and file jointly, then you may think that your income will be taxed at a 24% flat rate for federal income tax. That is not true because it is actually taxed at different rates: the first $19,050 is taxed at 10%, the next $77,400 is taxed at 12%, and the remaining amount up to $165,000 is taxed at 22%. Instead of a flat 24%, you'd end up paying about 17% overall federal income tax rate. This simple calculation didn't consider even basic deductions ($12,000 for singles and $24,000 for married couples filing jointly), so when you apply all your qualified deductions, your actual federal income tax would be less.

Misunderstanding of Deductions

Speaking of deductions and before I go further, I want to briefly point out how they work, as I sometimes hear people saying things like they want to get a bigger house for tax deductions. When someone says that, I feel like I hear he/she wants to buy something that is not necessary only to get credit card reward points. Of course, tax deductions are more valuable than credit card rewards, but not spending (therefore more saving) is inarguably better than any tax deductions. In a simplified example, let's say you incur $10,000 extra expense that is deductible by moving to a bigger home and your tax rate is 25%. Then, your actual tax saving from the $10,000 deduction is about $2,500. Does it make good financial sense to spend $10,000 to save $2,500? I don't know about you, but I would rather not spend $10,000, pay $2,500 tax, and save $7,500, instead. If your income tax rate is higher than that, say 30%, your tax saving will be $3,000. If your tax rate is lower at 15%, your tax saving from the same $10,000 deduction would be worth only $1,500.

You should also know that your deductions may have no tax saving effect, depending on your deduction and filing status. For example, if your total deductions are under $24,000 and you're filing jointly with your spouse, you may not get any tax savings because $24,000 is what all married couples filing jointly get in the basic deduction (2018). My point for this section is that you should consult your tax advisor to understand tax implications *before* you buy or sell properties.

State Income Tax

State income tax varies somewhere between 0%-13%, depending on which state you live, filing status, and the income. For your state income tax rate, visit BankRate.com (*State Tax Rates*).

There are currently seven states with no state income tax: Alaska, Florida, Nevada, South Dakota, Texas, Washington, and Wyoming. And residents in New Hampshire and Tennessee pay state income tax only on interest and dividend income, but not earned income. California currently has the highest state income tax rate at 13.3%. The warm weather is not the only reason that many retirees move to places like

Florida and Texas. If you are living in one of the seven states with no state income tax, your income will be subject to either or both payroll taxes and federal income tax, depending on the type of income.

Example of Taxation

Let's take a look at a simplified illustration of how earned income of $100,000 is taxed. Social Security tax and Medicare taxes are 7.65% in total, federal income tax is calculated using appropriate brackets, and a flat 5% is used for state income tax. Also, $24,000 is used for basic deduction for joint filers before income taxes are applied.

Taxes	Taxable Amount	Tax
SS + Medicare (7.65%)	$100,000	$7,650
Federal (gradual)	76,000	8,739
State (5%)	76,000	3,800
Total Taxes		$20,189

All other deductibles are ignored for simplicity, and states may have different standard deductions that are different from the federal one. If the couples' income were from rental properties, it wouldn't be subject to SS and Medicare taxes of 7.65%. If their income is from working, meaning it is earned income, and the couples have contributions on 401(k), deductible IRA, or HSA, the tax would be further reduced. If the couple's income is from rental proprieties, not from work, and they live in a state without a state income tax, their tax liability would be even lower.

Based on the tax liabilities calculated at the time of tax filing, you'd get a refund if you paid more than what you owe, but you'd pay extra if you paid less during the tax year. It is an overly simplified example to show the basics of how taxes are calculated. Consult your tax advisor for your tax estimation or any tax-related questions.

Long-term Capital Gains Tax

As you know, different types of incomes are taxed differently, and people with earned income (from working) end up paying more dollars in taxes than those with the same amount of ordinary income (rental income, short-term investment profits, etc.). Although the extra payroll taxes on earned income are necessary to be eligible for workers' future Social Security and Medicare benefits, and people without earned income cannot contribute to tax-advantaged retirement accounts, that is something that people with ordinary income only do not have to pay. There is another type of income that is taxed at even lower tax rates than ordinary income: long-term capital gains.

To qualify for a lower long-term capital gains tax rate, you must hold the investment for at least one year and one day before selling it for profits. If you profit from investments that is held for one year or less, the gains will be subject to a higher ordinary income tax.

There are three tiers in capital gains tax: 0%, 15%, and 20%, depending on your taxable income. If you, single, have taxable income of $38,600 ($77,200 for joint fliers) or less, your long-term capital gains tax rate is 0%. If your taxable income is $425,801 ($479,001 for joint filers) or more, your long-term capital gains tax rate is 20%. All income that's between these two rates is subject to 15%, but capital gains tax due is calculated at staggering rates as in federal income tax calculation. People with long-term capital gains from real estate investment may be allowed to defer their tax liabilities if reinvested in another property. Profits up to $250,000 ($500,000 for joint filers) from sales of a primary home is exempt from capital gains tax, if the owners lived in it for two years out of the past five years. Be sure to see a tax advisor *before* selling investments for profits.

Wealthy individuals often have more investment income than earned income, effectively paying lower tax rates than the rest of the people whose income is mostly from work. That is how Warren Buffet, one of the richest people in the world, was able to pay only 17% on his $40 million income for the 2010 tax year, as he wrote in a column in The New York Times (*Stop Cuddling the SuperRich*). The average tax rate of 20 employees in his office was 36% for that year, he said. He asked in the article if it is fair for superrich people like him to pay a lower rate when so many Americans are struggling to make ends meet. What do you think?

AMT (Alternative Minimum Tax)

Alternative minimum tax (AMT) was initially designed to have the wealthy pay their fair share of taxes. Essentially, tax liabilities are calculated in two ways: first using regular tax rules like the example we saw and second, using AMT rules. Once people's regular tax liabilities are calculated using a federal and state income tax schedule, the AMT is calculated based on that data. A list of deductible items are first added back to adjusted gross income (AGI) under regular tax rules. Then, different exemptions and tax rates are applied, depending on one's filing circumstances. Unlike the federal income tax schedule that has seven brackets, AMT has only two rates: 26% and $28%. If the AMT is less than regular tax liability, then no AMT is paid. If the AMT is more than regular tax liability, the difference is paid on top of the regular tax liability. In other words, whichever higher should be paid. If you want to learn more about the AMT, visit IRS.gov (*Alternative Minimum Tax (AMT) Assistant for Individuals*).

Unlike its original intention of having a small number of highly wealthy people pay their fair share, the AMT has been affecting mostly upper-middle-class workers. That is because while regular income tax rules (taxable income, deductions, exemptions, etc.) have been indexed with inflation, the AMT has not. Also, because of the way the AMT is calculated, people with high earned income living in a state with a high state income tax are hit the hardest. Up until 1990, less than one million people were affected by the AMT, but it is expected to affect roughly five million taxpayers in 2017, according to TaxPolicyCenter.org (*What is the AMT?*). The Tax Cuts and Jobs Act that is effective starting 2018 tax year addressed this issue by raising exemptions and permanently indexing them for inflation. Now AMT is expected to affect considerably fewer people going forward.

You may wonder, by the way, how Warren Buffet was able to pay only 17% of his $40 million income in 2010? That is mainly because the majority of his income was from long-term capital gains, which is taxed at lower capital gains tax rates, which is 20% maximum. He also donated a large amount of money and deducted it from his income.

Sales Tax

We pay sales tax when we buy most goods and services, and the tax revenues are generally used to run state and local governments. A sales tax rate is flat and can widely vary depending on states and cities. In Missouri where I live, the state sales tax is 4.225% (2018). Cities and counties impose their own sales and use tax on top of the state sales tax, allowing two neighboring cities to have different sales tax rates. The average total sales tax in Missouri is 7.89%. Find out what your state's average sales tax rate is at TaxFoundation.org (*State and Local Sales Tax Rates in 2018*).

Not all retail items are taxed at the same rate. Most states have low sales tax on grocery items, while some items such as gasoline, tobacco, and alcohol products, are subject to special taxation called excise tax. An excise tax may be either a percentage or a flat dollar amount and is included in the price of goods. The federal government, states, and each municipality can impose its own excise tax on different products, causing consumers to pay different prices for the same item in neighboring states or cities.

There are five states that don't have state sales tax: Alaska, Delaware, Montana, New Hampshire, and Oregon. That doesn't necessarily mean residents in those states pay less tax in general because sales tax is only one of the ways to collect revenue for state and local governments to operate. Residents may pay higher income tax, property tax, excise tax, or higher price tag for state universities, etc. Alaska that has neither state income tax nor sales tax heavily depends on revenues generated from natural resources such as oil and gas operations. States that have overall lower tax rates (and low tax revenue) often lack good public services: it takes money to provide public services such as good libraries, schools, roads, parts, etc.

Property Taxes

Property taxes are imposed on local properties. It can be real estate property such as homes and buildings, or it can be a personal property such as cars and boats. Revenues from property taxes are primary sources for operations of counties, cities, school districts, public water system, etc. Tax rates vary by jurisdictions, but they are typically 1-2% of property values. States with no income tax or sales tax tend to have a higher property tax rate. If someone defaults on property taxes, the local government can place a lien on the property and eventually put it up for sale to collect the unpaid taxes.

Unlike other taxes previously mentioned, a property tax amount may be contested based on assessed values. You know, two houses of the same size and structure in the same neighborhood can be sold for different prices for many reasons, particularly depending on updates. If you feel that your assessed value (property tax) should be lower than other comparable homes in your area, contact your local tax office and ask how you can appeal it. Your local government office is likely to have that information on its website, though. I've seen some people taking pride in paying higher property tax than their neighbors, thinking their house is "better." The amount of your property tax does not necessarily mean that. Feel free to contest it if your tax is higher than your neighbors with a similar property. Make a careful comparison based on the size of homes and lots, year built, upgrades, etc., and find a property(s) that has lower tax (assessed value) than yours. You should be able to find your neighbors' tax record on your local government website or a real estate website such as zillow.com. Once you have information that supports your claim, file it at your local government office and argue for the fairness of taxation.

Estate/Gift Tax

An estate tax is paid when assets are passed onto someone else after one's death. It is sometimes called as "death tax" by opponents. In spite of its infamous nickname and many people opposing it, it affects only a small number of very wealthy people in America who could leave more than $11 million ($22 million if married) as of 2018 (IRS.gov - *What's New - Estate and Gift Tax*). That exclusion amount has more than doubled from $5.49 million in 2017. According to Tax Policy Center (*Who Pays the Estate Tax?*), about 11,000 individuals dying in 2017 were expected to have large enough estates that require an estate tax return. Among those people who are required to file, only about 5,000 would end up paying estate tax after deductibles and credits, the organization says. Since the exclusion amount has more than doubled from 2017's, only about 2,000 individuals are estimated to be affected by this tax in 2018, according to The Washington Post (*3,200 Wealthy Individuals Wouldn't Pay Estate Tax Next Year Under GOP Plan*).

Gift tax is paid if one gives more than the exclusion amount, but the amount is accumulated to the maximum estate exclusion, which is currently over $11 million. There's an annual exclusion amount that doesn't even require tax filing, which is $15,000, and married couples can give up to $30,000 (2018). There is no limit on the number of people to whom one can give in any given year. For example, as a married couple, you and your spouse can give $30,000 to 100 people, which is $3 million in total, without having to file for gift tax return. If you give the same amount to three people, $1 million each, you do have to file it but won't have to pay any gift tax until the total gift amount reaches over $22 million, which is the lifetime exclusion for married couples (2018). Gift/estate taxes are paid by the people who give, and individuals can receive gifts without any tax consequences. The gift/estate taxes discussed here are federal taxes, and your state may have a separate gift/estate tax rate with own exclusion amounts.

Since this book is mainly for people who would not be affected by these taxes, I'll not discuss this topic further. If you are concerned that you may be subject to gift/estate taxes, consult your tax professional, estate attorney, and financial planner. Effective estate planning requires teamwork.

Tax Problems?

I sometimes see people who think they are so smart that they can "trick" the IRS and pay little or no tax. None of them is a tax professional or works in the field, so I don't know what makes them think that. What I *can* say for sure is that they are not "tricking" anyone but themselves by not doing their taxes right. A fraudulent tax report is a serious crime and the consequences are worse than whatever amount that they think they are "saving."

Hiring professionals will initially cost you, but you can save much more money and trouble for many years to come. At the very least, file your taxes on time and do not lie. Claiming more deductions than you are eligible or omitting income will slap you hard with years worth of back taxes, penalties, and interests. If you see a tax preparer who claims that he/she can somehow "reduce" your taxes without verifying your eligibility, please do yourself a favor and walk away. Regardless who prepares your tax filing, you are responsible for proving the accuracy.

Chapter 11
ESTATE PLANNING

Estate planning is not just for the rich. It is something that anyone with assets should consider to help his/her surviving family save time and money after death.

1. Importance of Estate Planning
2. Probate
3. Will
4. Health Care Directives
5. Trust

Chapter 11 | ESTATE PLANNING

Importance of Estate Planning

Do you know what happens to your assets when you die? Without designating who gets what in advance, all of your assets will go through a legal process called probate before being transferred to the rightful heirs. This process can take a long time and be costly. Many people incorrectly think that estate planning is for the rich, but not having an estate plan, assuming you own something that is worth money, is like an invitation for your loved ones to fight after your death, in my opinion. You'd be surprised how many family members, who have had a good relationship, suddenly fight over money after their loved one's death. Even if there's no fight among heirs, taking some simple steps can mostly avoid probate, saving time and money before assets can be transferred.

Probate

Again, probate is a legal process of identifying rightful heirs and transferring assets with clear title. It follows state laws and any debt owed by the deceased will be first paid in the process before transfer. All personal assets go to probate unless beneficiaries and ownership are designated before death. If you die with a house and a car in your name only, for example, both properties go through probate. According to Nolo.com, typical probate for "routine" estate with a gross value of $400,000 can easily cost over $20,000 (*Why Avoid Probate?*). Assuming your house would end up being transferred to whomever you'd have wanted anyway, the associated fees still must be paid. If you don't leave enough cash behind, your heir(s) may have to sell the house to pay for the probate court fees. If there are disagreements among heirs, a lawsuit can be filed, causing lengthier and costlier process. Even if there won't be any disagreement between your heirs, probate becomes public information that anyone can later see, which is yet another reason to have an estate plan.

Simple Ways to Avoid Probate

For most people, their "routine" assets can easily be cared for without any complex estate planning. For financial accounts, you can designate a beneficiary(s) by signing a simple document at your financial institution. For example, you can put your spouse as a primary beneficiary and your child as a secondary beneficiary. That means you want 100% of your assets in that account to go to your spouse after your death. If your spouse is deceased at the time of your death, your money will go to your child. If you want your spouse and child to get an equal share, put both as primary beneficiaries with 50% each. In banking, this form is called TOD (transfer-on-death) or POD (pay-on-death).

The basic idea is the same for real estate and personal properties like a house and a car: you can list your spouse or whoever you want the property to be inherited to as a joint tenant with right of survivorship (JTWRS) at a local government or DMV office.

Tenants-in-common (or tenancy-in-common) is a type of joint ownership that does go through probate after the owner's death: because it does not have a survivorship clause, it is treated as sole-ownership. It is commonly used in business ownership, which can be sold separately from the other owners. It is also used in a property owned by unmarried

Chapter 11 | ESTATE PLANNING

couples when one contributes more than the other and wants to give his/her ownership to someone else after death. If you have more than "routine" assets such as a business ownership with partners, you should consult an estate attorney.

There are other types of joint ownership, depending on where you live and how you want to jointly own properties. For more information and the pros and cons of each ownership type, visit Investopedia.com (*5 Common Methods of Holding Titles on Real Property*).

Things to Consider in Joint Ownership

This simple and free or low-cost process of adding joint owner(s) with a right of survivorship and designating beneficiaries will allow your assets to directly pass to your heirs, avoiding probate, but please understand the consequences of granting joint ownership to someone else. The joint owner(s) on your property have the same right as you, meaning they may be able to borrow against it or sell your property. Most buyers and lenders will want all the owners to sign in such events, but there are cases in which one owner being able to borrow against property without consent from the other owner(s). Also, if your joint owner has personal debt, the creditor may be able to put a lien on your property. Thus you should consider potential risks before adding anyone as a joint owner(s) of your property. If you want to avoid such potential risks, you can place your property in a trust. Consult an estate attorney if you have any questions regarding joint tenancy and owners' legal rights.

Also understand the differences between joint owners and beneficiaries: joint owners have the same right as you, but beneficiaries do not. If you put your son in your bank account as a joint owner, instead of TOD (transfer-on-death, which is beneficiary designation), he can withdraw money from your account without telling you. If you want someone to help you make payments without granting ownership to your account(s), consider power of attorney (POA) for that purpose and designate a TOD/POD.

Creating joint ownership also can cause gift/estate tax consequences, depending on the value of your assets. As of 2018, individuals can give/inherit a lifetime total of about $11 million without any gift/estate tax consequences. Double that amount for married couples. If you have substantial assets, including business ownership or have complex family dynamics, then you should consider more in-depth estate planning with a professional(s).

Will

You can create a will that directs who gets your assets after your death. Unlike many people think, a will is not necessarily a legally binding document when it comes to assets and inheritance. It is more of a "wish list" or "recommendation" on how you want your assets to be distributed after you are gone because beneficiary designation and ownership titling overrule what you say in a will. For example, suppose you put your daughter as a joint tenant with right of survivorship (JTWRS) on your house today. Then, you write a will later directing your house be sold and proceeds equally divided between your son and daughter. Your daughter gets the house 100% after you die.

All personal assets that are solely owned by the deceased without designated beneficiaries will go to probate. A valid will will be respected at the probate court, but it won't prevent surviving families from contesting it, which means they can legally fight to get more than what the will directs. If your will directs that all your assets go to your son, then your daughter who has the same legal right as your son is likely to contest. Of course, not all families fight over money, but why leave room for a fight if you can help it? Do what you can to prevent potential conflict amongst your surviving loved ones and minimize probate assets. Someone may not be happy with your prearrangements, but at least you are not leaving an invitation to fight. Your will is an excellent tool to direct what to do with residual personal assets such as furniture, bags, and jewelry. Without it, all of your probate assets may be sold and distributed among rightful heirs according to your state probate laws.

One thing that is legally binding in a will is child custody. I recommend all parents draft a will to designate a legal guardian(s) for their minor child(ren) in case of their premature death. If you and your spouse are leaving separate wills, be sure you both put the same person as a guardian to avoid a future conflict in case you were to die simultaneously.

Your situations may change after writing a will. Then write a new one, revoking the old one(s), and let people know of its existence. I recommend using an estate attorney to have your will prepared, but if money is an issue, you can write one from scratch, with two witnesses signed on it to be validated in most states. You can appoint someone you trust as an executor of your will so she/he can overwatch that your wishes are carried out according to the will. For more information on wills, visit AARP.com (*10 Things You Should Know About Writing a Will*) and Nolo.com (*Wills FAQ: What You Need to Know About Wills - The Most Basic Estate Planning Document*).

Health Care Directives

Document for Your Medical Wishes

Health care directives document your medical wishes in case of you not being able to make your own health care decisions. It may be called by different names such as advance medical directives, living will, declaration, advance directives, etc., depending on your state. See what it is called in your state on Nolo.com (*What Health Care Directives Are Called in Your State*). Regardless of its name, states usually provide this document for free, so people can prepare it while they can. In this document, you can state in advance if you want to be resuscitated in case of heart failure, tube-fed, mechanically ventilated, etc. when you can no longer make your own decisions. You may also express if you want your organs to be donated and if you want your body to be cremated or buried.

Power of Attorney for Health Care

You can select a power of attorney (POA) for health care and have that person, called an agent, carry out your health care related wishes. You can choose an agent as a part of your health care directives or in a separate document and grant him/her as little or as much power as you wish to make health care decisions on your behalf. Writing down your specific wishes on the health care directives and giving the residual decision-making power to your agent is recommended. Your agent's power dies when you die unless you grant durable power of attorney

(DPOA) for health care. So if you want your agent to also make decisions for your funeral arrangements, grant a DPOA for health care. Once you have these documents prepared, give a copy to your loved ones, doctors, financial adviser, and other people involved.

Consequences of Not Having It Prepared

I know, people don't want to think about their mortality, but no one wants to make life or death medical decisions for their dying loved ones, either. Think about it: how would you feel to have to tell the doctor(s) not to tube-feed or resuscitate your mother or father? If you and your parents had a conversation previously about this kind of situation, then the decision should be easier. If there's no document prepared by your parents before they became incapacitated, however, there's room for disagreements amongst family members. Do you remember the Terri Schiavo case that spurred a national debate over right-to-die? Terri Schiavo had a cardiac arrest and fell into a vegetative state in 1990. Her husband and her parents had a lengthy legal battle over medical treatments and the removal of her feeding tube until she died in 2005. Enormous medical and legal costs aside, I cannot imagine that is what Ms. Schiavo would have wanted. It could have been easily avoided if she had had a simple living will prepared.

I also want to share my story of my father who passed away in 2015. While living, and especially after my mother passed away after several months of suffering from cancer in 2006, my father often told me that he wanted to die "clean." He elaborated it by saying that he did not want to have any surgery or eat or breathe "unnaturally." Knowing of this document, I helped him prepare it and had my siblings sign as witnesses.

When he had a stroke and was taken to a hospital one day in February of 2015, the doctor in the emergency room asked me about surgery. I told the doctor what my father's wishes were, to which he said that he would have wanted the same for himself if he were in my father's situation. My father passed away peacefully and "naturally" within 24 hours of the stroke, just the way he wanted. My siblings and I are forever grateful for him to save us from having to make difficult decisions for him.

As I mentioned earlier, most states provide this form for free, so have it prepared while you can. At the very least, talk to your loved ones about this critical topic. I know it is a tough subject, but it is a conversation that needs to be had with your spouse, parents, siblings, and adult children, while you can. Please understand that it does get easier once you start. If you can't initiate this conversation, have your financial adviser help you. Read more information on advance health care directives on WebMD.com (*Advance Directives*).

Trust

A trust is a legal document that holds assets or is waiting for assets to be poured over in the future for the benefit of the designated beneficiaries. Think of it as a complex will that is legally binding. There are three parties involved a typical trust: a grantor, trustee, and beneficiary. The party that creates a trust and puts assets into it is a grantor but can be called by other names such as a settlor, trustor, or trustmaker. The party that manages and distributes the assets according to the trust document is called a trustee, and the one who receives the benefit is called a beneficiary(s).

A trust can be either revocable or irrevocable. The grantor of a revocable trust maintains control/ownership over the trust assets and can later cancel the trust. In a revocable trust, the grantor is responsible for income tax on the profits, if any, while in an irrevocable trust, the trustee is responsible. The assets in a revocable trust are included in the deceased's estate and are vulnerable to creditors, but they do not go through probate.

On the other hand, a grantor of an irrevocable trust does not have control over the trust assets and cannot cancel the trust once it is established. Assets in an irrevocable trust are no longer owned by the grantor, so his or her estate will not include them after death. The irrevocability protects the assets in the trust and the beneficiary(s), if the grantor has creditors that may otherwise be eligible to claim the assets. In case of either or both the beneficiary has debt or is in the process of divorce, the irrevocable trust assets may or may not be subject to claims from the beneficiary's creditors or the divorcing spouse, depending on how the trust is set and managed.

Who needs a trust, anyway? Generally speaking, if you want to "control" your assets after your death, you need a trust. For example, if you have minor children or a disabled family member who needs care after you are gone, you should create a trust and direct how the assets should be managed and distributed. If you want to create a legacy that can benefit your descendants for generations to come, a trust can help you achieve that goal. If you want your surviving spouse to benefit from your assets until death, but you want the remaining assets to go to a charity or anyone of your choice, a trust can do the job. Or if you simply want to avoid probate while maintaining the control of your assets until death, you can utilize a living trust.

Again, a trust is a legal document that overrules directives of a will, helps your assets avoid probate, and allows you to control the money after death. There are many types of trusts, and one can be as long as you want it to be with highly detailed instructions. Identify what you want and work with a team of an estate attorney, tax professional, and financial planner, as they have different parts to play in effective estate planning.

Chapter 12
ACHIEVING FINANCIAL STABILITY

Financial stability requires seeing a holistic picture of where you are now, where you want to be, and how you can get there. It is a lifetime process that needs cooperation from all family members. It also requires one to realize his/her limits and effectively utilizing professionals.

1. Financial Stability
2. Six Steps of Financial Planning
3. Five Numbers You Should Know
4. Ten Rules for Financial Health
5. Advice by Age

Financial Stability

We all know why financial stability is so important. But what is financial stability, anyway? It is your financial resilience to withstand financial stress. Will you be able to handle unexpected expenses such as car repairs, short-term unemployment, occasional emergency medical expenses, etc.? Will you be able to maintain your current lifestyle after retirement? If you are living paycheck-to-paycheck, like most Americans, one emergency can pull you into a financial crisis, making it very difficult to get back on track. Without enough savings, retirement can put you in poverty overnight. No matter how much money you make now, you are not financially stable if you (your family) don't have means to sustain the current lifestyle in case of expected and unexpected life events. Achieving financial stability is a process of increasing your financial resilience, and it requires the following steps to reach your goals effectively.

Six Steps of Financial Planning

If you work with a qualified financial planner, which I recommend, you will go through five or six essential steps in comprehensive planning together. If you do it without a professional, you can start from step 2.

1. Establishing a Relationship

It is critical that you and your financial planner first clarify expectations and responsibilities for each party. You both need to have a clear understanding of services, fees, and the duration of the professional relationship. Don't hesitate to ask questions to the adviser, and honestly answer the questions that you are asked. If you're married, be sure to include your spouse throughout the process, unless you intend to exclude him or her. It will be difficult or impossible for you to achieve your financial goals if you both are not on the same page.

2. Gathering Data and Defining Goals

Financial planning involves all aspects of your finances including savings, investment, and all spending. Without knowing the ins and outs of clients' finances, what an adviser can do to help his/her clients is inherently limited. Hence, be prepared to share all your financial data including personal expenditures and tax records with your adviser. Define what your financial goals are. Be specific in what you want with a time frame. Also, discuss your risk tolerance level with securities market ups and downs. Not clarifying your financial goals and comfort level on the market fluctuation can lead to a big problem down the road for you and the adviser.

3. Analyzing and Evaluating Financial Status

Once your financial adviser has all your financial documents and understands your goals, she should be able to come up with an action plan to achieve your objectives. If she thinks your goals are not realistic, she should let you know and help you revise them. Unless you requested limited counseling, she should present you an overall financial picture, including, but not limited to, net worth, cash flows, insurance analysis, retirement projection, and investment strategies.

4. Reviewing Adviser's Recommendations

Fully understand your adviser's recommendations and see if they are realistic for you to implement them. If the adviser recommends to reduce your weekend outings to half and stop paying for your adult child's phone bill to increase savings, for example, see if that is realistic with all things considered. Raise any concerns to the adviser and revise goals if necessary. If your adviser uses terms that you are not familiar with, do not hesitate to ask for an explanation.

5. Implementing the Recommendations

Once you and your adviser agree on the plan, it is time to implement it. Having a great plan means nothing if actions are not carried out, so thoroughly implement the recommendations. There shouldn't be any confusion on responsibilities for each party and time frame. Explain to your family what you are doing and have them involved in the process, as achieving financial stability requires teamwork from everyone affected.

6. Monitoring

Situations that can affect your finance may happen as time goes by. Your income and expenditures may change, or your assets may not grow as you anticipated. Children grow up, and family dynamics may change. Your financial plan should be monitored periodically and modified if necessary. I recommend this monitoring process once a year or when any life event that affects your finance occurs, whichever comes sooner. If you're close to retirement, say within five years, twice a year is recommended. Once a change needs to be made in your plan, go back to step 2 and continue the entire process, as it is a lifetime process. For more information and educational materials on the financial planning process, visit LetsMakeAPlan.org, a website run by the CFP Board (*Learning Center*).

Five Numbers You Should Know

No matter how good your financial planner is, you should know basic pictures of your finance, as you never know if the adviser will be there to help you during your lifetime. Here are five numbers that I think everyone should know:

1. Net Worth

Net worth is a snapshot of how much you have at any given time. You can add up assets and deduct liabilities to know your net worth. The assets should be listed at fair market value as of the calculation.

Assets
- Current market value of home (zillow.com)
- Current value of investments
- Money in bank accounts and CDs
- Value of your car(s) (Kelley Blue Book)
- Business interest
- Other assets and personal valuables (jewelry, collectibles, etc.)

Liabilities
- Loans (mortgage, auto, student, etc.)
- Credit card debt
- Other personal debt

Some people prefer to exclude their car and personal items from this calculation because it is not likely that they would sell those personal properties for money as long as they live. If you do include personal properties/belongings, however, be sure to use their market values for resale, not the purchase price, because that is what you'd get if you were to sell them today. Your net worth will be negative if you owe more money than the total current value of what you own. If so, don't be disappointed and calculate it next year. Hopefully, you'll see your net worth grow each year. What's your net worth as of today?

Net Worth: $_____ as of ___/___/_____

2. Emergency Funds

I cannot emphasize enough on the importance of having an emergency fund, as it is a financial cushion that you can fall on for unexpected expenses. To understand how much emergency funds you need, first know your monthly expenses. Write down your essential living costs such as mortgage/rent, other loan payments, insurance premiums, utility bills, foods, etc. Don't include discretionary spending such as eating out or travel. The amount of necessary emergency funds depends on your circumstances. For example, if you are married and both you and your spouse are working in a steady job with similar income, then you may be OK with only a few months worth of funds, but if you are the only wage earner in your household, you should save at least six months worth of emergency funds that can cover your essential living expenses. For seasonal workers and small business owners with fluctuating income, you'll need more. You can adjust the emergency funds as your situation changes. How much emergency funds do you need and how much are you saving?

Emergency Funds Necessary: $_____

Monthly Saving: $_____

3. Retirement Funds

Know how much you need at retirement to keep your lifestyle and how much you need to save to achieve that goal. This amount also depends on many things, but it is generally recommended to have at least 8-10 times your annual income by the time of your retirement. Go back to Chapter 5 Retirement Planning if you need help. How much do you need at retirement and how much do you need to save to reach that goal?

Amount Needed at Retirement: $_____

Necessary Monthly Saving: $_____

4. Financial Costs

As I keep emphasizing throughout the book, seemingly small financial fees can significantly reduce your overall retirement assets. They are like small cracks in a boat: If you don't diligently examine every corner to fix them, your likelihood of safe sailing (financial stability) will be lower. Know all the following financial costs by heart, and use a separate sheet if you need to.

Loan Interest Rates

Mortgage: _____% Auto: _____%

Student Loan:_____% Other: _____%

Credit Card Interest Rates

Card 1: _____% Card 2: _____% Card 3: _____%

Monthly/Yearly Maintenance Costs

Bank 1: _____ Bank 2: _____

Investment Account 1: _____ 2: _____ 3: _____

Annual Investment Costs (or %)

Account 1: _____ Account 2: _____ Account 3: _____

Other:

5. Credit Scores

As I explained earlier, bad credit can cost you a lot of money in many ways throughout your life. You should know your scores and take care of your credit as if it is a large sum of cash. What are your current FICO scores from all three credit bureaus?

Equifax: _____, Experian: _____, TransUnion: _____.

Ten Rules for Financial Health

The following rules are just "common sense" that has been said many times by many financially wise people. These points have been discussed and empathized throughout the book, but I believe they are worth summarizing at once.

1. Have Emergency Funds

Need I say more?

2. Never Say No to Company Match

If you are offered an employer match in your retirement plan, take it. For example, if your company offers a 4% match in the condition of your 6% contribution, not saving 6% is the same as you saying 'no' to 4% bonus.

Even if the required minimum contribution seems impossible for your current situation, I sincerely hope you try it first. You can reduce the savings rate once you realize that the savings rate is not fiscally possible. At the very lease, start with 3% contribution and *automatically* increase it by 1% each year.

3. Be afraid of Credit Cards and Debts, But…

It is so easy to fall into a debt trap. Do not use credit cards if you don't have enough cash to pay in full each month. If you already have credit card debts, prioritize in paying off the ones with higher interest rates first. Try to avoid taking new loans, even student loans, if possible. Understand that focusing too much on paying off loans or being debt-free can also be a mistake if it means no or lack of saving for retirement. You do need to balance between reducing debts and saving for retirement to effectively grow your wealth.

4. Save 50% of Windfall

If you get a bonus, raise, tax return, inheritance, or win a lottery, save at least 50% of that. It is not too much to ask to save half of "free money," is it?

5. Talk About Money

The undeniable reality is that we will never be free from money as long as we live, and too many people are financially suffering. We treat this national crisis largely as a private issue and don't openly talk about it. For any problem to be solved, we first must be aware of it. Unless you're from a very wealthy family, chances are that many of your loved ones are also worried about their financial future not knowing what to do. Many of them may have sleepless nights worrying how they could ever retire. Why don't we talk about this financial problem and see if we can help each other? The fact that you are reading this book tells me that you know way more than most Americans on what to do to achieve financial stability. Casually share how you are saving taxes by saving for retirement and protecting your assets from general creditors. Talk about the danger of credit cards and debts like you talk about food or home renovation. Give a book on personal finance for birthdays and holidays, instead of stuff that may get thrown away next year. I understand that this can be a sensitive subject, but even briefly mentioning that you've raised your retirement savings by 1% will get other people thinking, don't you think?

6. Talk to Your Children about Money

I know this may seem redundant in reference to the previous point, but I believe it deserves its own section. As parents, we all want our children to be happy, but can we really raise them to be happy when we're struggling to make ends meet and afraid of our financial future? Children can understand way more than many parents assume, so talk to them about the reality. Teach them the difference between "wants" and "needs" from an early age. There are many children's books on money for different age groups, read them with your children. If and when they ask about how much you make, welcome the question and tell them the truth. "Shielding" (a.k.a. lying to) the children from the truth about money serves no one in my opinion. If you lead your children to believe that you are financially better off than you actually are, you're missing a great teaching opportunity about life, which will later lead them to face reality the hard way. Include your children in budgeting for family events such as shopping, family travel, education savings, and your retirement planning. Take your children to see a financial planner when they get their first job.

Even if you're lucky enough to be wealthy, please teach your children that money needs to be earned and how many people are suffering to make ends meet. Your children won't be happy, no matter how much money they have if they don't learn to appreciate what they have. Besides, people who don't understand other people's suffering cannot become a good leader, whether in family or career, in my view.

7. Helping May Hurt

We all want to help our loved ones, but our "love" can actually hurt the very ones we want to help or can become a boomerang and hurt our own finances. If you're constantly helping working adults with their bills, for example, you need to see if you're somehow contributing to their inability to be financially independent. If you keep lending money to someone who does not pay back as promised, you may be actually "teaching" him to ignore the importance of credit. Even if none of the above applies and you want to help your loved one by lending money once, do so with what you can afford to lose, in case it is not paid back. In other words, assuming the money you lend to your loved one is not getting paid back is the only way to protect your relationship and finance, in my opinion, although you shouldn't tell the person what you think.

I won't repeat the danger of co-signing, but if you ever do co-sign for anyone, have the borrower pay you, and you make the payments to the lender. It is the only way that you take control of your credit and help the borrower build his/her credit.

8. Expand Your Lifestyle Slowly

One of the first things that many people do when they make more money is to expand their lifestyle, and that is not smart. You can easily buy a bigger house or a nicer car any time, but you cannot easily downsize once you expand your lifestyle if you have payments. What good does more income do if you don't feel financial freedom? Focus on saving and increasing your financial resiliency, and take your sweet time buying material things. You'll have a more fulfilling life by focusing on your financial freedom, instead of material things.

9. Know When to Pay

I've spent a lot of time explaining how fees can hurt your asset accumulation throughout the book, but please understand that not investing or seeking help because of fees can jeopardize your long-term financial stability. Good financial professionals can help you save, grow, and protect your money way more than the fees you pay them. Utilizing professionals for your advantage is a good investment.

10. Pay Yourself First

Always pay yourself first, no matter how much you make. Although the required savings rates may vary depending on your situation and age, plan to save about 15-20% of whatever you make. Setting up automatic saving/investing is the key. Your life is much too precious to work endlessly only to fill other people's pockets (credit card companies, lenders, utility companies, etc.). Save for yourself *before* sending out any payments.

Advice by Age

If You Are a Teenager

Congratulations! The fact that you are reading this book shows that you want to learn about personal finance, and it will put you way above most people.

If you grew up in a family who commonly talk about saving and investment, I hope you know how lucky you are. I see too many people with a professional job who never learned the importance of saving and investing, not to mention the power of compound interest. Do not assume everything you hear from your friends and family is correct, however. There are many smart people who have been investing for a long time but don't understand the importance of diversification, how much they pay in fees, how those fees affect their asset accumulation, etc. Continue your learning and verify what you think you know is true. Open a Roth IRA and save 20% as soon as you make any money and invest in well-diversified index funds with low costs. There's no minimum age requirement to open a Roth IRA account, and you can open one with the money you make from irregular jobs such as babysitting or private tutoring.

If you grew up in a household with modest income where the word 'investment' is a foreign language, double congratulations! By choosing to read a book like this, you've just put yourself in a place that can take you much farther than your family ever did. You are also in a unique position where you can positively influence your families even at this age. Keep learning and share your knowledge and this book with your siblings, cousins, and even parents. I hope you'll work hard to get the necessary education to get a good job, but if you have to settle, please understand that you can always improve your finance with good planning. More importantly, time is on your side: starts saving the day you first get paid. No matter how much you want to help your financially struggling family, make sure you save for yourself first. You cannot meaningfully help anyone if you too are on a sinking ship, metaphorically speaking.

If you are college bound, take control of your finance even if you still get help from your family: it is your life. Be on top of the entire process, including FAFSA, CSS Profile, and other financial aid applications and scholarship searches. Student loans are a fast-growing national problem that affects all ages, so try your best to minimize college education costs (loans). Talk to your parent(s) about how your education would be paid for. Also, carefully choose your major. Angela Duckworth, a renowned psychologist, says in her famous book, *GRIT*, that for people to have a sustainable happy life, they need to do what they are passionate about, the job needs to pay their living wage, and the work should be beneficial to others. Think hard to find out what that may be for you as you apply for college.

Finally, vote as soon as you are eligible. You may think politics are for adults, but they affect you and your family way more than you may realize now. You wouldn't let a stranger come into your house and control you and your family's life, would you? By not voting, you're essentially allowing politicians and other people who vote decide rules that directly and indirectly affect you and your family's health and money such as health insurance rules and student loans. See the real issues beyond the political jargons that some incompetent politicians want you to see and vote for the best interest of you and your family.

If You Are 20-Something

Start building your emergency funds with 10% of your income *and* save another 10% for retirement from whatever money you make. If you cannot pull off 20% savings, do what you can but increase it by 1% each year for both until you reach the threshold. Once you have a minimum of three months worth of emergency funds, allocate the savings for retirement.

If you are dating someone, see if that person has a healthy spending habit (and good credit) before you get into a serious relationship. One of the main reasons that couples fight is over money, so find out if you two are compatible before falling in love, if possible. Before you get married, have an open conversation about personal finance. Exchange all information including, but not limited to, savings, debts, credit scores, income, health condition, and anything that can affect your finances and marriage. By the way, please do not get into debt for your wedding: it is such a foolish way to start a new life, in my opinion. If you have assets that you want to protect from potential divorce, say you have a family business interest, or you inherited a great deal of wealth before marriage, then have a prenuptial agreement signed. Once you are married, make financial decisions and manage assets together. Even if one partner manages all financial matters for whatever reason, the other one should minimally know where, how much, and in whose name their assets are.

If you have anyone who is financially dependent on you, get life insurance and prepare a will designating a guardianship for your child(ren), in case of your premature death. See a financial planner to have a blueprint to achieve your financial stability.

If You Are 30-Something

You may have family and more obligations by now, yet this is an age that you still feel very young and retirement seems a thing of too far in the future. If you don't prioritize savings, however, you will see yourself regretting very shortly. You should be minimally saving 15-20% of your gross income for retirement, including your employer match in a retirement plan. By your mid-30s, you should have at least twice your annual income saved, according to Fidelity.com (*How much do I need to save for retirement?*).

Thirty-something is a good age to be practical and care less about what other people think of you. If you're not saving for your retirement or your child's education, don't even think of buying everyone gifts for Christmas, for example. Then, speak about it, so other people will stop giving you gifts that may not be appreciated or used much anyway.

Also, you are old enough to ask your parents if they are well-prepared for their retirement. It may feel awkward asking such "personal" questions, but their financial instability will likely to become your problem down the road. (What are you going to do if your old parents don't have money for their medicine or food?) Help yourself while you can by encouraging your parents to take care of their finances.

If you are a parent, start a parent "match" program with your child. If she saves her money in her bank account, match it 100% or whatever you feel comfortable with. If she wants to withdraw money for things that she "wants," but not "needs," take the match portion away plus a 10% penalty. You can have exceptions for things like donations or education-related expenditures. Have your child write the rules, so she'll clearly understand them. Once the savings hit a certain amount, move a large portion into her education account and start talking about investment and college costs with her. I think this is an excellent way to teach children the excitements of saving/investing that will help them for a lifetime.

If You Are 40-Something

Your clock is ticking fast. By your mid-forties, you need at least four times your annual income saved. Unless you've done what is recommended from an early age, see a financial planner without any delay. Make your retirement saving a top priority even over your children's college saving. Utilize all tax-favored accounts including a retirement account through work, IRA, and HSA.

Know how much you need to support your current lifestyle, how much your Social Security and pension benefits will be, and have an action plan. Planning to work until you drop is not realistic or a plan. If you know there's a low possibility of achieving your retirement goal, start thinking of alternatives now.

Update beneficiaries on your accounts, especially if your family situation changed. I've seen a widow being left with almost nothing because her deceased husband forgot to change the beneficiary on his retirement account, which was his single largest asset, from his ex-wife who he had divorced decades ago.

Chapter 12 | ACHIEVING FINANCIAL STABILITY

If your children start making money, encourage them to contribute to their 401(k) and IRA. There are no rules that the money has to be earned through payroll to open a custodial or guardian Roth IRA account. You can open one for your minor child as long as she makes money from working, whether it is from babysitting or selling lemonade in your front yard, but allowance for doing house chores doesn't' count.

If You Are 50-Something

The retirement storm is out the window. By mid-fifty, you should have saved at least 6-7 times your annual salary to minimally keep your current lifestyle after retirement. This amount is separate from Social Security benefit you expect to receive at retirement. If you haven't, you should cut expenses as if you are in a financial emergency because you are in one. Without taking such a drastic measure, you're quickly running out of time to have a stable postretirement life. Please save all you can. Desperate times call for desperate measures.

One good thing with your age, 50 or older, is that you are now allowed to save extra in your tax-advantaged retirement accounts. For a 401(k), you can save an extra (called catch-up) $6,000 and up to a total of $24,500 ($25,000 in 2019). With an IRA, the catch-up is $1,000 with a total of $6,500 ($7,000 in 2019). If your spouse works, have him/her do the same with the retirement savings. If not, she/he can still contribute into a spousal IRA. The catch-up contribution for an HSA is also $1,000, and you can save up to $7,900 for a family plan from age 55 ($8,000 in 2019).

Think beyond money and start planning what you'd do after retirement. For those who make it to full retirement age, there's a good chance that they'd live over 20 years after retirement. What would you do to keep your mind and body healthy?

If You Are 60-Something

By the time you retire, you should have at least 8-10 times of your annual salary saved. If you haven't retired and haven't saved enough, save all you can. Don't give up, as anything saved is better than nothing. See if you can work until 70, increasing your Social Security benefits by 8% per year after your full retirement age. Consult a financial planner how to maximize your Social Security benefits years *before* you (and your spouse, if married) apply. If you know your current lifestyle cannot be sustained after retirement, try to downsize now. Start living on whatever amount you'd get at retirement. Sell your home before you're forced to do it later, or see if you can rent out some portion of it.

While all debts can have dire financial consequences, there are only a few that can follow you till death even after bankruptcy. Federal student loans are one of them, and there is a disturbing trend of senior citizens with an increasing amount of student loans and Social Security garnishment. The garnishment amount is capped at 15% of the Social Security benefits, but it can still be detrimental to those who already are struggling to get by. Please fully understand the consequences before co-signing a student loan for your loved ones.

One of the common mistakes that people at this age make is to stop investing in equity securities. Unless you have enough funds to support your life until death, your money needs to grow even after your retirement. Keeping all your investments "safe" will bring another set of risks: either your money will lose value to inflation, or you'll run out of it while living. It is critical that you continue to invest while balancing between all risks as long as you are alive.

Update your will, medical advance directives, and beneficiaries on your financial accounts. Create a trust if you need to. Talk to your loved ones about your final wishes, including medical treatments in case of your incapacitation and funeral arrangements. It is never an easy subject to discuss, but it gets better once you start talking. More importantly, your loved ones will appreciate it very much later.

If You Are 70 or Older

Complete what was discussed in the previous section, regarding updating documents and talking about your living wishes with your family. If you're still working, continue to save what you can, unless you don't need to. You can keep contributing into your 401(k) even after 70, as long as you're working. Once you hit 70 ½ years of age, it is time to worry about the required minimum distribution (RMD) from your pre-tax retirement accounts. Penalties for failing to take your RMD are monstrous at 50%. Thus, make sure you get it taken care of by talking to your financial planner or financial institution. If you're contributing into your 401(k) and don't own more than 5% of the company you're working for, you may be able to delay RMD from the current 401(k), but not from IRAs and old 401(k)s, if any.

Consolidate or simplify your assets, if possible. Make a list of your assets and keep it with other financial documents and living will for your loved ones to easily find later. If and when you help your loved ones financially, try to do it in a way that can help them long-term. For example, open an education account for newborn babies instead of buying a fancy crib, and gift down payment for newly married couples instead of paying for their wedding.

It is also time to reflect on your life. Share how you got there with young people around you so they can learn from your success and failures. If you are barely making ends meet, please know that your life is way more than what you saved or didn't save. Do not let money define you or your life and be the positive influence on people around you with dignity and a big smile. ❖

About Author

Misook Yu, CFP®

Misook Yu was born and raised in South Korea. After high school and working for several years and saving money, she came to America for college. She studied programming at a community college where she met her husband, Terry.

After living in America over two decades and realizing that being frugal and making "good income" is not enough to achieve financial stability, she went back to school to study personal finance at age 40. At the University of Missouri St. Louis, she majored in finance while taking an extra personal financial planning course for CFP® studies. She graduated with the highest honors, Summa Cum Laude.

Misook is currently working as an independent financial planner while writing columns for The Korean-American Journal in St. Louis, and online blogs, focusing on public education and financial awareness. When not working as a financial planner, she teaches a Korean class at a community college and helps student robotics teams in underserved areas with her husband and their children.

Made in the USA
Columbia, SC
23 February 2019